THE LEADERSHIP BLUEPRINT

THE LEADERSHIP BLUEPRINT

BECOMING THE ARCHITECT OF YOUR LIFE AND WORK

Tess Cox and Daniel Klawer

ISBN-13: 9781540644671
ISBN-10: 1540644677

We dedicate this book
to
intentional people
who choose
to
design their lives
through
being lifelong learners.

TABLE OF CONTENTS

OUR PHILOSOPHY:

Designing a blueprint for your life and work will lead you to build a great life and career.

The Components of the Leadership Blueprint - The 5 C's

Character – The Foundation

A person of character knows who they are and why they do what they do. They are able to build trust with others through their integrity, trustworthiness, and honesty.

Competence – Pillar Number 1

A person of competence understands the reality of their skills and knows how they bring value to their relationships and work with their expertise. They are able to build trust with others through their well-known capabilities, qualifications, and experiences.

Consistency – Pillar Number 2

A consistent person is known for being reliable. They are able to build trust with others by creating predictable structures, systems, and measurable results. They also have the ability to stabilize situations.

Creativity – Pillar Number 3

An influential person has the ability to create strong relationships. They are able to build trust with others. They are able to think of new ideas and process input with others. Their solutions produce excellent outcomes for the good of themselves and others.

Confidence – The Protective Covering

A person who possesses confidence personally and professionally builds trust with others. Their quality of communication is high, and they excel when resolving conflicts. They are able to influence others through listening, gathering feedback, and collaborating with them to find solutions for best results. Confidence is fully realized through the development of the first four C's.

This book has four parts:

Part 1 – <u>CONSTRUCTION 101</u>

With short daily readings, during the 1st four weeks, you will be introduced to the foundation and three pillars that hold up the life you lead: Character, Competence, Consistency, and Creativity.

Character focus builds your foundation as you make the choice to lead yourself first. **Competence**, **Consistency**, and **Creativity** are the pillars of your leadership, which are supported by your foundation. As you focus on the daily readings you will build your self-awareness in each of these areas, which will ultimately build your Confidence in your ability to manage your own behaviors.

As you study these first four C's, you are given the opportunity to pause, reflect, and write about your own thoughts, new knowledge, and insights.

Confidence is built when we live with Character, Competence, Consistency and Creativity. It is not built in a vacuum. Confidence is built on the practice of knowing who you are, why you do what you do in life and work, and how you are capable of creating a lifetime of meaning. It is the roof or covering with which you seek to protect everything that you have worked so hard to achieve.

Daily readings for Character, Competence, Consistency, Creativity and Confidence are provided for you in Part 1. You may choose to read the content on a daily basis and participate in the exercises for personal and practical application. Or, you may choose to read all the way through and go back and discover how you would like to apply your learning. It's up to you.

It's All About Your Choices

Daily Reading
Introducing The Foundation of Your blueprint
Character

Introducing The Pillars That Rest on Your Foundation
Competence
Consistency
Creativity
Confidence
Construction 101:
    Continue the 5C's of Leadership Blueprint Daily Reading

Part 2 – <u>DESIGNING YOUR LEADERSHIP BLUEPRINT</u>

Change requires a plan. With a 1 week focus on one of the 4 C's – Character, Competence, Consistency, and Creativity – we will guide you to create and implement four strategic action plans to build your self-leadership and ability to manage behaviors in each area. You will have the opportunity to design your own blueprint for excelling in life and work. Part 2 is designed for you to make use of over and over again as you choose new areas of focus to build new strategies.

It's All About Your Strategy

Putting your foundation and pillars into practice:

Character

Competence

Consistency

Creativity

Part 3 – <u>TRACKING YOUR LEADERSHIP PROGRESS</u>

Charting progress is the only way to know what works and what doesn't. During these final four weeks, you will choose one area of focus upon which to build your confidence. You will document your progress. During this time, it is important for you to understand which of your new habits are working well for you and which are not. As you assess your outcomes, you will realize where you need to adjust your strategies and blueprint. As with all habits, these will take practice, time, and patience.

It's All About Measuring Your Results:

The protective covering of confidence that helps you thrive

Confidence

Part 4 – <u>THE LEADERSHIP BLUEPRINT: REFLECTION</u>

Reflection is your chance to "walk around the jobsite" that is your life. You wouldn't build a structure and never walk around it. You'd want to know how it's progressing. The ability to reflect is a unique opportunity; we are the only life form on the planet with it.

Reflection helps you to see both the subtle and not-so-subtle changes in your life. As you begin to lead yourself well, take regular time to reflect. Ask yourself the following questions:

- What is working well for me?
- What would be helpful if I were willing to change my way of thinking in order to approach situations and people differently?
- What isn't working, no matter what I think or which approach I use?

Good, healthy reflection will cause you to ask the difficult questions that help define a true reality. If you want true change, it is imperative that you listen to the answers that come to you as you reflect.

The core of who you are, longs to live in the reality and fullness of light and truth. The daily denial of chaos, crisis, challenges, and continuous difficulties keeps your true, core reality from living in the present. You may tell yourself, "Things are not that bad at work." Or, "Things will eventually get better in my relationship." But is this reality?

Reality is waiting for you to reflect and act! Healthy reflection helps you develop the best decisions, choices, and movement forward for your best outcomes. Reflection also gives you the pleasure to enjoy what you have worked hard to attain.

You are the leader of your life in all ways … a time of reflection will bring you more gratitude for the life you are living, or it will redirect you toward the life you long to live – one that is meaningful and true for you.

Before you begin your new journey of learning, we recommend that you log onto our website, www.the-leadershipblueprint.com for more resources.

Our website also provides you the opportunity to sign up for a "Leadership Blueprint" coach. Our coaches are trained to enhance your learning experience by creating a weekly dialogue with you.

It's All About Your Transformational Change

PREFACE

During the summer of 2013, Tess asked Dan to describe what he thought made an extraordinary salesperson. She had been asked to train a group of salespeople and needed expert advice from Dan. She listened while he explained his process for training and instilling excellence among members of his sales team.

As she communicated her takeaways from his insight, she said, "Dan, you have the blueprint that every person needs to succeed! And this blueprint is not just for salespeople." So, Tess and Dan began a journey together to design the blueprint of leading your life well by using Character, Competence, Consistency, Creativity, and, ultimately, Confidence. These "5 C's" are the starting place for you to understand as you become the lead architect of your life and work and before you seek to lead others.

Each of the 5 C's is one element of a sound structure for experiencing personal and professional success, including career choices and solving complex issues and conflicts. Here is the exciting part: Unlike a home or building that has a final build-out plan, this blueprint allows you to *constantly* expand, remodel, and upgrade the structure that is **your life**, because you are the architect.

As you reflect on your outcomes, you have the opportunity to decide what is working well in your life and career. You also can reflect on when and if you get stuck. It takes a special skill to step outside of yourself and examine what needs to be adjusted and where you might need new solutions. Further, you can reflect on what decisions need to be made to begin moving in a different direction.

Reflection gives perspective and guidance for moving your life towards leading yourself forward.

PROLOGUE

On May 19, 2014, a YouTube video went viral. The video was of a commencement speech delivered by Adm. William H. McRaven at the University of Texas. Almost three million viewers have heard his core message, summed up in the memorable line:

"If you want to change the world, start off by making your bed."

The Navy SEAL veteran recalled, "If you make your bed every morning, you will have accomplished the first task of the day. It will give you a small sense of pride and it will encourage you to do another task and another and another. And by the end of the day, that one task completed will have turned into many tasks completed. Making your bed will also reinforce the fact that the <u>little things in life matter</u>. If you can't do the little things right, you'll never be able to do the big things right. And if by chance you have a miserable day, you will come home to a bed that is made – that you made – and a made bed gives you encouragement that tomorrow will be better."

Every day needs a blueprint. This choice of making your bed in the morning is akin to laying the foundation of your day. Everything you do will be built upon this single, simple choice and action.

If nothing else, you'll have a tidier bedroom.

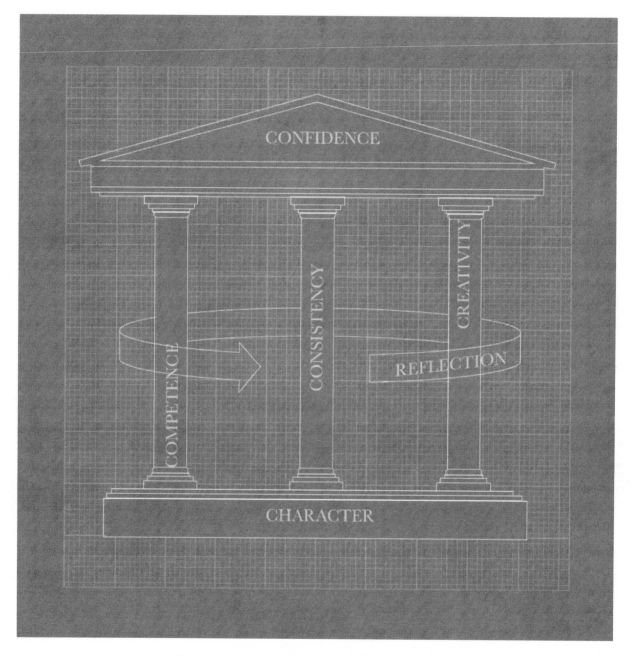

"LIFE IS THE SUM OF ALL YOUR CHOICES."
ALBERT CAMUS

> "Life can be exciting and challenging –
> when we make an everyday choice
> to lead and live a life that matters
> we experience a meaningful
> and influential life."
> TESS COX AND DAN KLAWER

Your learning, practice, and implementation of these leadership components – the 5 C's – will help you to develop and influence the way you live, your philosophy, your choices, and your purpose by the way you:

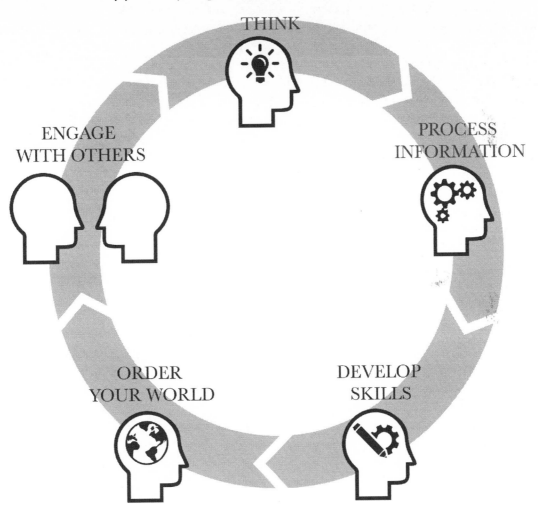

- **<u>Think</u>** - using your intellect, which shapes your paradigm
- **<u>Process information</u>** - using your personality
  you process information with an ability to be conceptual and/or with an ability to gather facts and data
- **<u>Develop skills</u>** - using your expertise
- **<u>Order your world</u>** - using developed, positive, and affirming habits
- **<u>Engage with others</u>** - using your emotional understanding of yourself and others

You lead your own self every day, in each of the areas mentioned above.

Who you are influences your way of thinking and how you process information.

Why you do what you do impacts the way you develop your skills and habits.

How you create meaning in your life reflects your ability to be engaged and to form relationships with others.

Your choices have a strong effect on all of your outcomes, every day.

Do you know who you are? Every day, who you choose to be in any moment, no matter what the circumstances, matters. Who you are is not dependent on where you are, who you are with or what you are doing in life and work. Who you are is how you create your value system, which infuses your life with meaning, both personally and professionally. It is how you choose, every day, to grow and develop as a leader. Throughout the book we make no distinction between your personal and professional lives. Your choice to learn and grow as you create the blueprint for leading your life is present in and will affect both spheres of that life.

Every choice you have ever made has created the reality of the life you lead today. When you take your last breath on this Earth, the same will hold true.

This very moment is your opportunity to begin altering the course of your life by designing your blueprint and you can START NOW!

**You matter,
and we want you to thrive both
in your learning and in leading yourself well.**

PART 1

CONSTRUCTION 101

IT'S ALL ABOUT YOUR CHOICES

> **"Excellence is never an accident.**
> **It is always the result of high intention,**
> **sincere effort, and intelligent execution;**
> **it represents the wise choice of many alternatives –**
> **choice, not chance, determines your destiny."**
> ARISTOTLE

Why commit to this process of being the lead architect of your life and work? Because the slightest sustained improvement in your daily choices and habits can have a profound effect on the long-term outcomes of your life.

Creating the Blueprint:
The repetition of your good choices supports satisfying outcomes. Good outcomes create a momentum of success. The positive and healthy behaviors that lead you to success are worth repeating. This cycle of success creates your ability to thrive in your life and your career.

Blogger James Clear writes about using behavioral science to improve your performance and master your habits for a healthy life. Below is one of his blog posts from The Huffington Post that perfectly illustrates the phenomenon of incremental improvement:

"In 2010, Dave Brailsford faced a tough job. No British cyclist had ever won the Tour de France, but as the new General Manager and Performance Director for Team Sky (Great Britain's professional cycling team), Brailsford was asked to change that.

"His approach was simple. Brailsford believed in a concept that he referred to as the 'aggregation of marginal gains.' He explained it as 'the 1 percent margin for improvement in everything you do.' His belief was that if you improved every area related to cycling by just 1 percent, then those small gains would add up to remarkable improvement.

1

"They started by optimizing the things you might expect: the nutrition of riders, their weekly training program, the ergonomics of the bike seat, and the weight of the tires.

"But Brailsford and his team didn't stop there. They searched for 1 percent improvements in tiny areas that were overlooked by almost everyone else: discovering the pillow that offered the best sleep and taking it with them to hotels, testing for the most effective type of massage gel, and teaching riders the best way to wash their hands to avoid infection. They searched for 1 percent improvements everywhere.

"Brailsford believed that if they could successfully execute this strategy, then Team Sky would be in a position to win the Tour de France in five years time.

"He was wrong. They won it in three years. In 2012, Team Sky rider Sir Bradley Wiggins became the first British cyclist to win the Tour de France. That same year, Brailsford coached the British cycling team at the 2012 Olympic Games and dominated the competition by winning **70 PERCENT** of the gold medals available.

"In 2013, Team Sky repeated its feat by winning the Tour de France again, this time with rider Chris Froome."

JamesClear.com/marginal-gains

This blog post also depicted a fantastic visual representation of what the aggregation of marginal gains would look like over time. A person's level/quality of results over time looked like this:

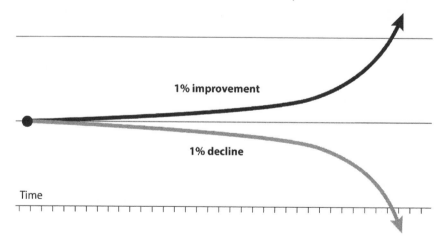

Aggregation of marginal gains on choices we make

In the beginning, there is basically no difference between making a choice that is 1% better or 1% worse. In other words, it won't impact you very much today, but as time goes on, these small improvements or declines compound and you suddenly find a very big gap between people who make slightly better decisions on a daily basis and those who don't.

1% improvement

1% decline

Time

The amazing part of this phenomenon is: If you observed two people, each representing the black and gray lines, at the outset, their activities would appear very similar. One percent is not a significant change.

However, when you look at the results of that one percent effort compounded over time, it becomes clear that this is a nearly effortless way to become more skilled, more powerful, and more effective, just one percent at a time.

This is exactly like compound interest, only instead of an investment in your financial success, this is an investment in your personal and professional success, and its small increments will pay off greatly over time and create more and more sustainable outcomes.

> **"Success is a few simple disciplines, practiced every day;**
> **while failure is simply a few errors in judgment, repeated every day."**
> JIM ROHN, ENTREPRENEUR

HOW TO READ PART 1 OF THIS BOOK:

Reading Part 1 is a daily commitment to your pursuit of personal well-being and professional development. Week One will be a longer read as we define the foundation and pillars of the structure of who you are, why you do things, and how you create meaning in your life. The following weeks will be shorter and should require no more than 15 minutes each day. We have included space in each section in which you can write your own thoughts and respond to questions for full engagement and interaction. You have the freedom of choice to write as much or as little as you prefer throughout your reading and learning.

This four-week focus will increase your personal understanding of YOU – the inner workings of your perceptions, thoughts, reactions, likes, and dislikes. As you build your self-awareness you will be able to begin to respond to others with a higher level of appropriate openness and integrity.

This segment will challenge you to evaluate and think about your behaviors. You will learn to assess what habits are working well for you and what habits need adjustment for better outcomes. This improves your ability to self-manage your own behaviors and be more responsible for leading yourself in a sensible and self-regulating way.

At the end of the book's 90-day program, we trust you will not only be inspired, but will also have experienced a transformational change. You will have gained the skills to create your leadership blueprint as the architect of your life – having incorporated into your life a skill set that we refer to as a leader of your emotions and intellectual abilities.

Enjoy your journey!

WEEK 1 / MONDAY

CHARACTER
THE FOUNDATION

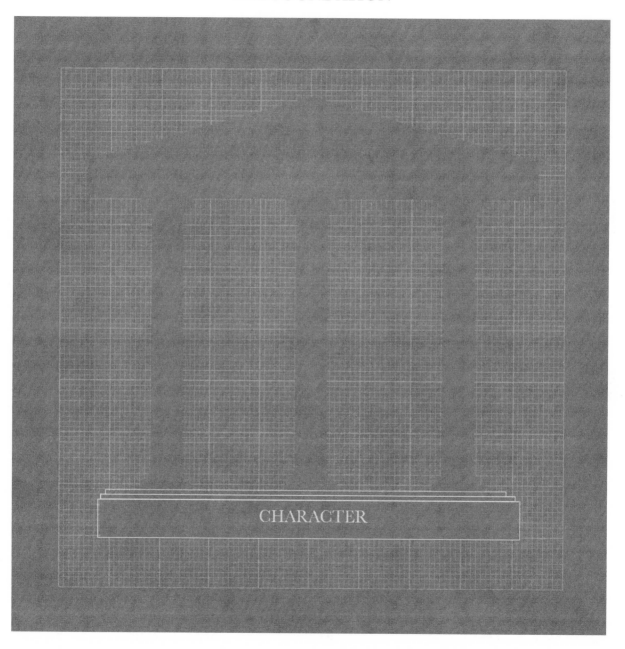

CHARACTER

A person of character knows who they are and why they do what they do. They are able to build trust with others through their integrity, trustworthiness, and honesty.

> **"Sow an act, reap a habit.**
> **Sow a habit, reap a character.**
> **Sow a character, reap a destiny."**
> CHARLES READE

What does this quote mean to you?

_____

_____

_____

_____

Your actions and habits lead you along a path that drives your existence and carries you to your ultimate destiny. We want your destiny to be a meaningful life.

Creating the life you want to live requires your best intentions and actions. We will begin your journey focused on the importance of your **Character**, as it is the foundation of every choice you make.

Envision yourself walking into a room full of people. Every time you walk into a room, you bring your character along. In every interaction with others, you bring your character. It is your greatest resource and single most important asset in living a meaningful life.

If you were an architect designing a structure, where would you begin? Certainly not with the windows, walls, or roof. Every well-built structure begins with a solid foundation. We know, as we have both lived in earthquake-prone Southern California. When the Northridge earthquake struck in January 1994, it was a frightening experience. As we assessed the damage to our homes, we were amazed that there was no "real" structural damage! We learned that the solid foundations of our homes had saved our personal belongings, the structures themselves, and possibly our lives!

It works the same way for you as you pursue the life you want to live: Character is the solid foundation upon which you build everything you do, and it will positively or negatively influence your life and its outcomes.

Business philosopher Jim Rohn said, "Everything affects everything else. There are some things that matter more than others, but there isn't anything that doesn't matter."

More than anything, character matters.

A healthy character brings:

- Peace of mind
- Self-assurance
- Trust from others
- Credibility
- Personal excellence
- New opportunities
- Increased wisdom

5

> "We are weaving character every day,
> and the way to weave the best character
> is to be kind and to be useful.
> Think right, act right;
> it is what we think and do that makes us what we are."
> ELBERT HUBBARD
> (NINETEENTH-CENTURY AMERICAN WRITER, PUBLISHER, ARTIST, AND PHILOSOPHER)

You may have further thoughts on why character matters to you. If so, write them here:

_____

_____

_____

_____

_____

_____

_____

_____

CHARACTER
Integrity Builds Trust With Others

"Whoever is careless with the truth in small matters cannot be trusted with important matters."
ALBERT EINSTEIN

Building trust with others and being a person of integrity, every single day, can be really tough! Why is it so challenging to be a person of character? Our paradigm is based on this thought: Integrity requires you to make a conscious decision to *be* this person – a person people trust. It requires you to know your true self and deliberately respond to all situations with integrity. We are not talking about being a person of character for just a day or two, or depending on the situation. We are talking about being a person of character every single day, no matter the situation.

There are no shortcuts to this process. Building your life with character will affect every person with whom you relate, so it needs to matter most to you.

Character continues to build or decline over time, as our lives get more and more complicated and require purposeful choices. As hard as it is to build character, it can be lost in the blink of an eye. The news, the workplace, and your community lack no shortage of stories about people who are no longer trusted. When they made a poor choice, the direction of their life changed – in some instances, dramatically.

- Think about the position you hold at work
  Your board, CEO, managers and co-workers expect you to be a person of integrity.

- Think about your personal relationships
  Your family and friends expect you to be a person of integrity.

- Think about your church, clubs, organizations, and teams of which you are a member
  Your fellow parishioners, team members, and other group members expect you to be a person of integrity.

A good question to ask is, "Where did I first learn about being a person of integrity?" For most of us, it comes from our family system. For others, the first exposure to integrity may have been experienced through school or work.

As early as we can remember, most of us were raised with a paradigm that character and integrity count – it was fundamental to our upbringing. For others, character and integrity may be qualities learned over a period of time or that came with maturity.

Building character, integrity, and trusting relationships is not as easy as flipping a switch.

People of character realize that everything they say or do really does matter. You (and every other person in your life) will choose to be either, honest and truthful, or not.

Different choices will lead you down very different paths with very different outcomes.

A Study in Character and Integrity

An interesting example of character can be seen in the 2002 movie "Catch Me If You Can," with Leonardo DiCaprio as Frank Abagnale Jr. and Tom Hanks as FBI agent Carl Hanratty. It was based on the true story of Abagnale, who as a young teenager faced the crises of his father's bankruptcy and parents' divorce.

As part of his coping mechanism, Frank began a series of cons, the first of which was as a substitute French teacher. From this successful con, he moved on to conning his way into being employed as a doctor, lawyer, and a co-pilot for a major airline, all before his 21st birthday! Abagnale was also a brilliant forger whose skill in check fraud netted him over $2.8 million in stolen funds.

Early on, Abagnale observed his father's way of "conning" people to do what he wanted them to do. His mother had her own plans for creating the life she wanted, which did not include his father. Abagnale's family system did not provide a strong foundation of character, so he went into survival mode to keep his life going.

As he conned his way through various jobs and forgeries, his life's "plan" was not sustainable (just as it was not sustainable for his father). Hanratty makes it his mission to bring Abagnale to justice. In the end, Abagnale is caught. Ultimately, deception and crime do not return the best dividends. When caught by Hanratty, Abagnale was jailed to pay the price for his crimes. He ended up serving the latter half of his sentence working with the FBI to help the agency spot and prevent check fraud. His life began to turn around when he accepted his responsibilities, addressed his character flaws, and increased his trustworthiness. Abagnale began a new life.

"Catch Me If You Can" is worth watching as a study in character and integrity. You may be thinking, "I'm no Frank – I'm not a con artist!" We know; we feel the same way. Yet, you need to ask yourself:

"Do I correct the person who gave me more change than what I was owed?"

"Do I log in the accurate number of hours that I worked?"

"Do I tell my spouse/partner how much the investment cost?"

"Did I tell my kids that I would take them out to play when I got home but didn't because I mismanaged my time?"

"Does my yes mean 'yes' and my no mean 'no'?"

These questions are meant to help you think about the choices you make every day that set you on the path toward integrity, trustworthiness, and reliability. It is quite probable that you are not going to con artist extremes. Still, daily you are faced with the option of being a person of integrity or a person of fraud. We are all imperfect human beings, and the gift of choice is an opportunity to choose integrity every day, in every decision.

Even in seemingly small choices, a lack of integrity begins to damage your self-image and undermine everything. In fact, small choices tend to be the most likely place for a lack of integrity to start. The practice of integrity expresses both inward-focused self-respect and outward-focused respect for others.

Dan's Opportunity to Own His Character

In November 2013 I was at a company sales meeting. Every quarter we get everyone together and talk about what we can do better as a sales team and how we can be better leaders in our company and industry.

I wasn't feeling well that day. I decided to go to the hotel restaurant and get a ginger ale to calm my stomach. On my way down to the restaurant I made the decision to check out of my room early due to not feeling well.

As I sat down and waited for the drink, an awful feeling materialized when I realized I had left my iPhone in my room. Not what I needed, and to increase my misery, I had a raging headache, which had me teetering on the edge of vomiting. Staggering back to my room, I saw the bed sheets were no longer on the bed, and no maid was in the room. I looked down the hall and felt a glimmer of hope when I found a maid. I asked her about my phone. She told me my maid had gone downstairs, and it was possible she took my phone with her. I was in terrible shape as I rode the elevator back to the lobby.

As I sat in the lobby nursing my ginger ale and hoping my phone would turn up, I had a stroke of very good luck. A man in a black suit walked up to me with a phone. He asked me, "Sir, is this your phone?" Relieved, I said, "Yes!"

Then he said, "Also, we found your sunglasses." He offered me a beautiful box that read "Prada." Immediately, I told him they weren't mine. If I hadn't been feeling like death, I would have laughed out loud. It's not everyday that someone offers you a free pair of $400 sunglasses.

For some people, a "free" pair of Prada sunglasses would have been enticing. I'm happy to say, they had no appeal to me because I was brought up with a framework of good character and honesty. Plus, I know the guilt that I would have felt if I had taken them for "free." In my blueprint of leading myself well, guilt is not going to lead me to positive outcomes.

When faced with tests of integrity:

- Listen carefully to what is being asked or said.
- Give yourself time to answer, pause and reflect.
- Ask clarifying questions before you respond.
- Think about the outcome you want, and focus on this outcome no matter what kind of pressure you feel.

This is CHARACTER: Knowing to do the right thing without hesitation or need to justify or mull over your decisions.

The greatest outcome of a successful blueprint for character allows us to create trusting relationships.

> " 'Integrity' comes from the same Latin root
> as the words 'integrated' and 'integer.'
> A person of integrity is when there is no gap
> between intent and behavior …
> when he or she is whole,
> seamless, the same inside and out."
> STEPHEN M.R. COVEY

<u>Write down three key things you have learned about character:</u>

1) _____
   _____
   _____

2) _____
   _____
   _____

3) _____
   _____
   _____

<u>Reflect and focus on your character.</u> <u>Write your thoughts about these questions:</u>

What would happen to your life, career, and relationships if you improved your character?

_____
_____
_____
_____

What problems in your life, career, and relationships would be solved if you focused on and improved your character?

_____
_____
_____
_____

In the areas of honesty, trustworthiness, and reliability, what do you need to change to become a person of character?

_____
_____
_____
_____

CHARACTER
Integrity Builds Trust With Others

You are what you think.
TODAY – Focus on forming and developing the following principles:

- **Be honest**
  A person others believe in.

- **Be trustworthy**
  A person who cares about others.

- **Be truthful**
  A person who speaks truth.

- **Be reliable**
  A person who is faithful and responsible.

<u>Read the above points at least three times today.</u>
What do the statements mean to you?

_____

_____

How will you incorporate their meaning into your daily interactions with others?

_____

CHARACTER:
On a scale of 1-5 (1 being low and 5 being high), assess the present quality of your character at work.

_____

On a scale of 1-5 (1 being low and 5 being high), assess the present quality of your character in your relationships.

_____

<u>WEEK 1 / TUESDAY</u>

COMPETENCE
Pillar Number 1

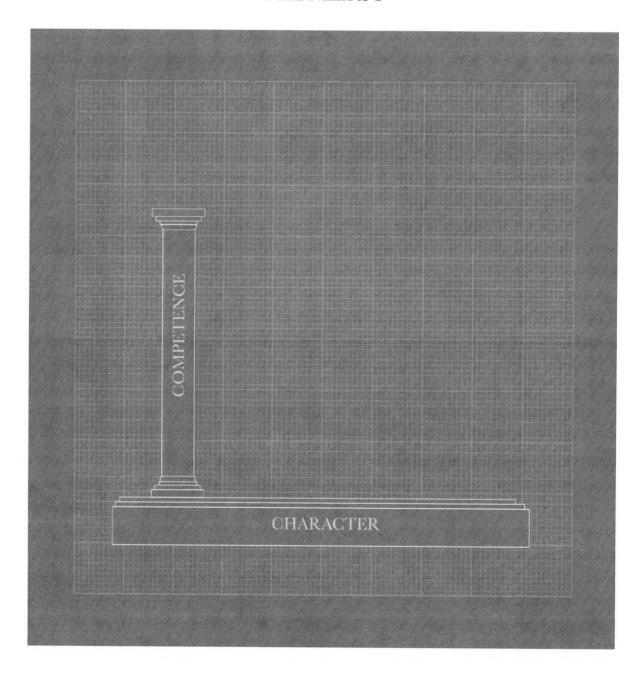

A person of competence understands the reality of their skills and knows how they bring value to their relationships and work with their expertise.

They are able to build trust with others through their well-known capabilities, qualifications, and experiences.

> **"Competence goes beyond words.**
> **It's the leader's ability to say it,**
> **plan it, and do it in such a way**
> **that others know that you know how –**
> **and know that they want to follow you."**
> JOHN C. MAXWELL

What is Competence?

Competence is the ability to:

- learn new things
- communicate with others
- prioritize what is most important
- act when you see an opportunity

Continuing with the analogy of a solid structure, competence is one of the three supporting pillars built upon your foundation. Competence is unique to each person and provides a critical element of support in creating a meaningful life.

What does competence mean to you? Write your thoughts below:

_____

_____

_____

We know that competence varies with each individual. Every day you use your competence in your life, work, and relationships, and it impacts your life and the lives of others. In fact, every person, born into this world is uniquely woven and intricately complex with natural capacities that have the ability to learn, grow and develop unique skills and talents – the family legacy of competence is within your DNA.

One of the very first competencies that you developed was the ability to walk when you were about 1 year old. It is safe to say that you have no memory of your early walking experience and yet, as we recall the smiles on our children's faces when they took their first steps – the look of "I'm conquering the world!" – it is priceless to realize the confidence children display when they realize they can walk competently. As a small child, your ability to learn how to walk was one of your greatest successes. So how could learning to walk be such a great achievement if you don't have any memory of the experience?

Walking requires intellect, coordination, skill, and, most importantly, a willingness to fall and get back up. It builds resilience in your physical, emotional, and psychological being. With each new step, you increased your competence and your confidence. To your parents' chagrin, it didn't take you long to figure out that your legs could do more than walk – they could run, climb too, and off you went! As you became more capable in your walking, and you required fewer failures of falling down on your face or plopping down with your feet out in front of you, your world began to expand with endless possibilities. You could walk anywhere! And, with practice, you learned to run!

It's time to have that experience everywhere else in your life.

Think about the most amazing places you have walked, climbed or ran in your life since then. What comes to mind?

_____

_____

_____

_____

_____

To this point, your life has had so many different possible outcomes because you walked through this door or out another. It is likely your competence has opened many doors of opportunity. It is even possible that doors have closed due to a lack of competence (a challenging reality)!

The more you increase your competencies with increased knowledge and intellect, new skills, developed talents, quality communication, and the seizing of new opportunities, the more your world expands with endless possibilities.

We understand that over the years the current developing landscapes of the world, your workplace, and your personal life look quite different from the landscapes of previous generations. We are faced with increasing complexity in the areas of diversity, multicultural dynamics, global opportunities, technology, and dispersed relationships. What continues to be critically and consistently important is the value placed on being a person of competence.

Just as you bring your character with you every time you walk into a room, you also bring your competence. In every interaction with others, your competence is noticed, and it matters!

The authors of "The Leadership Challenge," James M. Kouzes and Barry Z. Posner, tell us, "You cannot do what you don't know how to do, no matter how moral or noble the purpose." This is so true! Acquiring the competence for what you want to do in life will propel you to the results you desire!

We have found that when competence is fully present, others will see you as:

- genuine
- able to accomplish results
- committed
- a learner
- dedicated to improvement

"It is easier to do a job right than to explain why you didn't."
MARTIN VAN BUREN

"I am merely competent.
But in an age of incompetence, that makes me extraordinary."
BILLY JOEL

If you have further thoughts on why competence matters to you, write them here:

_____

_____

_____

_____

_____

_____

COMPETENCE
Learn – Unlearn – Reshape

"It's what you learn after you know it all that counts."
JOHN WOODEN

Learning is the ability to increase in knowledge and understanding through the process of study and experience.

Unlearning is the ability to question and discover, which leads you to let go of or remove past learning that is no longer effective for you. This is an important concept as clearing the past ineffectual learning, enables you to acquire new and productive knowledge and wisdom.

Reshaping is the ability to study new information in order to reimagine or refine existing thoughts, views, and paradigms.

Most likely, you began your journey of learning through your family system. You have a DNA of intellectual strengths, personal abilities, and unique talents. Your creativity and intellect led you to study different subjects in school, which was the beginning of the path upon which you now find yourself.

When you are driven to learn, humble enough to unlearn things that are not working, and courageous enough to reshape your views when presented with new information, you have the opportunity to go above and beyond the norm – to design and create the blueprint for your future.

Take a moment and reflect on three people who are good learners, humbly willing to unlearn, and courageous enough to reshape their views. They can be people you know personally or people you admire from knowledge of their work and competence.

Write their names below and why you see them as good learners, humble and willing to unlearn and courageous to reshape their views:

1) _____
_____
_____

2) _____
_____
_____

3) _____
_____
_____

Do you see these three as people who are able to address leadership challenges?
Are they able to formulate their own thoughts?
Are they able to grow in their views and opinions?
Have they developed philosophies that guide their lives with meaning and value?

Building Your Capacity to be the Kind of Person You Admire

When you have a drive to move forward, you will commit to finding the necessary knowledge. When you want to excel in life and work, you will pay attention and possibly "unlearn" the things that are not working for you. With new knowledge and the realization of what isn't working, you will be able to reshape your thoughts and views, giving you a sense of self-empowerment and influence. This will encourage you to do things differently and more competently. This competence will increase your ability to influence others. As you can see, one great skill leads to another.

As a consultant and coach, Tess has had the opportunity to influence the paradigms of her clients. Her best clients tend to be good learners with a desire to grow and become effective leaders who are able to make a difference in their roles and responsibilities. One important piece of learning is for her clients to understand the difference between leadership and management. A title or position does not automatically make one a leader. In fact, it is very possible to have a leader's title and not be a leader at all. Other people in the organization may not possess a title and yet be seen as very effective leaders. This often happens in companies where there is an absence of true leadership on the executive team.

When you have knowledge of the difference between leadership and management it makes a tremendous impact in your interpersonal leadership style and skill. Two key distinctions between leadership and management are:

- Leaders tend to focus on collaborating with others to define, and then effectively communicate, the "big picture" and vision to a larger audience. A leader will focus on goals and objectives to motivate and empower others for the good of the whole more than they focus on individual processes. They inspire those who follow towards future possibilities with clear organizational direction.
- Managers tend to focus more on the execution of systems and having people in the right positions to follow through a well thought out and planned strategy. The methodology and focus is on implementation with tactical execution. They are committed to the vision and determined to mobilize others to accomplish the projects or tasks at hand.

A leader is not void of being able to manage others and a manager is not void of being able to lead others. The two roles function differently. Both leadership and management are necessary to solve complex issues in life and business. So often, the challenge with management is that it is viewed negatively. Case in point: You've no doubt heard the word "micromanager." Yet, you'll notice the word "micro leader" does not exist.

Our goal is for you to consider yourself a leader, in your life and work, regardless of whether or not you have formally earned the title or position. You are more than a manager of your life and business. With all of the everyday details of living, you are a leader who is moving toward your vision with goals and strategy. From the moment you wake up in the morning, you lead yourself every day (you may not see yourself as a leader today and yet, this is our hope for you).

> **"Managers are people who do things right,**
> **while leaders are people who do the right thing."**
> WARREN BENNIS, PH.D.
> "ON BECOMING A LEADER"

In business, we need leaders and managers working together at their highest levels of competence to ensure the best outcomes. United leadership and management guide others to learn, unlearn, and reshape their views. This transforms organizational cultures and impacts effective decision-making for the benefit of the entire organization.

Tess' Client Learns Self-Awareness

In the winter of 2014 I had a conversation with a leader that I had recently taken through a nine-month coaching process. She commented,

> "I could not have navigated through my most recent leadership challenges if I had not learned how to build my own personal self-awareness, such as knowing my emotional triggers in a dialogue, in order to self-manage my own behaviors and responses."

Her desired outcomes were impacted by her willingness to learn something new, unlearn or discard what was not working for her, and reshape her paradigm about others, along with her approaches with them. Her response to others was not about being mechanical or superficial; it was about having the right perception, letting go of her past emotional triggers, and becoming the person she wanted to be in the present moment – fully present, engaged, and in charge of her emotions. She led herself well as she managed her emotions and did not allow for her emotions to be triggered within the conversation. And, she engaged with her highest level of knowledge and intelligence. As she led and managed herself well with emotional competence first, she was able to manage and lead the emotions and paradigms of others, which led to the best of outcomes for all – solving a complex issue with cross-functional teams.

Do you see yourself as a learner of yourself, first?

_____

What does learning about who you are mean to you?

_____

_____

"All readers may not be leaders, but all leaders ARE readers."
PRESIDENT HARRY S. TRUMAN

If you do see yourself as a learner, how many personal development / leadership books have you read in the past six months? (We trust this book isn't your first!)

_____

What kind of books are you reading? Write down the titles of three of your favorite books and why you are reading them:

1) _____
_____

2) _____
_____

3) _____
_____

What new information is important for you today for your personal learning and development?

_____
_____
_____
_____

What old information are you holding on to that you need to unlearn? (You may need to discard some past learning.)

_____
_____
_____
_____

What current information is necessary to help you reshape your paradigms?

_____
_____
_____
_____

The mind that continually grows and develops because of new ideas and new knowledge is the most valuable kind.

Three key things you've learned about competence:

1) _____
   _____
   _____
   _____

2) _____
   _____
   _____
   _____
   _____

3) _____
   _____
   _____
   _____

Reflect and focus on your competence:

What would happen to your life, career, and relationships if you increased and transformed your competence?

_____
_____

What problems in your life, career, and relationships would be solved if you focused on and increased your competence?

_____
_____

In the areas of learning, unlearning, and reshaping, what do you need to change to become more competent?

_____
_____

COMPETENCE
Learn – Unlearn – Reshape

You are what you learn.
    Today – Focus on your ability to hear and absorb information:
    <u>Ask yourself the following questions:</u>

- **What information is important for me to know today?**
  Be open to learning something new.

- **What information will help me to excel and do my best today?**
  Unlearn what is not helping you to move forward.

- **What new skills do I need to improve my relationships and work performance?**
  Reshape paradigms and build new strengths.

<u>Read the above points at least three times today.</u>
What do the statements mean to you?

_____

_____

How will you incorporate their meaning into your daily interactions with others?

_____

<u>COMPETENCE:</u>
On a scale of 1-5 (1 being low and 5 being high), assess the present quality of your competence at work.

_____

On a scale of 1-5 (1 being low and 5 being high), assess the present quality of your competence in your relationships.

_____

WEEK 1 / WEDNESDAY

CONSISTENCY
Pillar Number 2

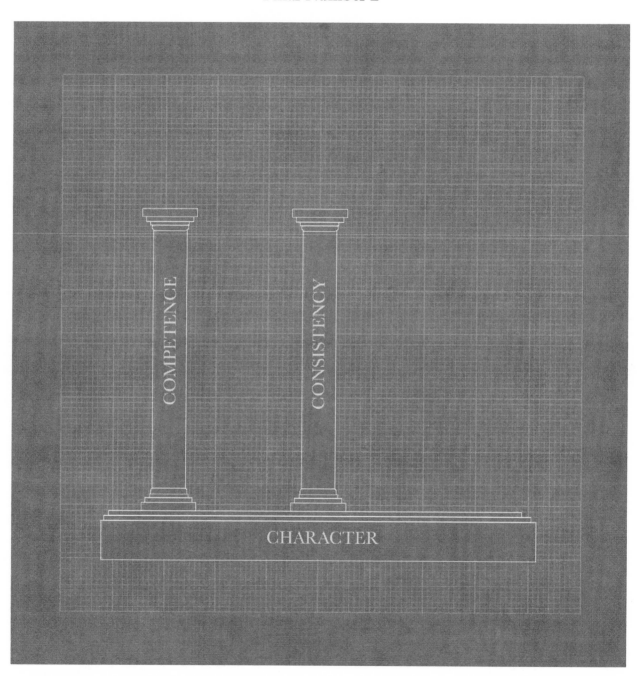

A consistent person is known for being reliable. They are able to build trust with others by creating predictable structures, systems, and measurable results. They also have the ability to stabilize situations.

"Embrace the hell out of personal responsibility."
COACH K (MIKE KRZYZEWSKI)

Tess Receives a Gift

A few years ago, I was coaching a group of sales and tech executives. One of the leaders was an excellent team builder. As we worked together, he said to me, "You've given me so many books to read on leadership; it's my turn to give you a book!" A few days later, I received a book written by Mike Krzyzewski – Coach K – called "Leading With The Heart." I respect and value both my client and Coach K's passion for their teams. Coach K is committed to a leadership blueprint that encompasses excellence in developing his teams and consistency is one of the areas he promotes for the best outcomes. Coach K believes that if his team will do enough little things in practice that simulate what will occur during a game, his team will position themselves to win every time.

Athletes can teach us about consistency

When we think about the world's top athletes, we are amazed at their ability to compete at the highest level. As spectators we enjoy cheering from our living rooms and talking about their abilities and conquests:

- "Did you see?"
- "What incredible skill!"
- "That win was amazing!"
- "I can't believe they could be so strong and talented!"

It's hard to imagine someone being so devoted to a sport or skill in their own life and work. But we like athletes' personal stories, which help us to see them as human. Yet their approaches to life, skills, and profession are not the norm.

Let's consider Olympic athletes:

- They make extreme sacrifices to be the athletes they envision themselves being.
- They use productive, repeated, and practiced habits that lead to success.
- They create consistency in their competent behaviors, which are exemplified throughout their performances.

These athletes have consistently practiced for so many hours that they have fortified their neurological pathways to communicate to every nerve ending and muscle fiber in their body, which remember every move needed to compete at the highest level. Athletes at this level may appear to be on autopilot. Yet, they are far from it; they are in an extremely consistent, complex mindset – they are "in the zone" of participating in their sport.

You can be in your zone, as well, in your field of expertise.

Productive, healthy, consistent, and even sacrificial habits matter – not just in athletics, but also in every aspect of who you are.

From the beginning, as you seek to lead and manage yourself first, we have encouraged you to focus on marginal gains, well-considered decisions, and consistent choices. A "paper published by Duke University researchers in 2006, found that more than 40 percent of the actions people performed [consistently] each day weren't actual decisions, but habits." Neurological impulses or patterns create a map for automatic behavior. You may think that each habit means relatively little on its own, but over time, you will begin to see that habits have an effect on your choices every day.

Reflect on the following:

- The meals you eat and the exercise you undertake affects your weight.
- What you say to your partners every morning before you depart for work affects your relationships.
- What you say to your children every night before you put them to bed affects their childhood memories.
- How you save or spend your money affects your retirement plans.
- The way you organize your thoughts and handle your work-life balance affects your health, productivity, financial security, and happiness.

Developing a Baseline of Consistency

Dan teaches the salespeople at his company a sales process that is entirely focused on the quality of consistency:

They learn to consistently see their customers every two weeks, on the same day of the week, and at approximately the same time of day.

This provides two key benefits for the salespeople:

The first is that prospects and customers become "trained" to expect the salesperson at a particular time. This expectation eliminates having to ask the salesperson to stop by as soon as possible to deal with a problem, take a new order, or handle some other imminent crisis. Because of the reduction in these types of interruptions, salespeople can be more efficient, and they actually end up seeing more customers in a single day than they would if they didn't have their customers "trained."

The second benefit is the credibility that this consistent routine provides.

Picture yourself at a party. At every social gathering, there tends to be people who attract a following. Some people are consistent as great storytellers, others tell jokes, and some people just possess raw charisma.

At this party, you see a group of people gathered around someone you don't know. Everyone is following the story and laughing. You can immediately tell that this person has some level of influence, even though you do not know them, you do understand there is a consistency at work as to who they are and who they attract to themselves. This understanding works similarly with the sales process.

The inference that the clients ultimately make, whether they intend to or not, is this:

"If this guy is calling on me consistently every other Tuesday at 10:00 a.m., and he never lingers, this must mean he is seeing someone else after me, and likely before me as well. He must have a full schedule!"

So, if Dan's salespeople do this correctly, the "client" can "see the group" of people without seeing the group. It's like magic. The consistent visit allows the salesperson to develop this social proof in a vacuum. The consistency of the visits begins to fascinate the customers, who infer that this salesperson is valuable, and they will be well-served to work with him.

Once this reputation is established, even with someone who is not yet a customer, it becomes easier to trust and ultimately buy from the salesperson.

Salespeople who understand this phenomenon that they can become this extraordinary person have a competitive edge in the marketplace.

Consistent Habits Are Key to Your Everyday Success

We want you to be known for your consistency. We want you to practice consistent behaviors. We know old habits can be dislodged and replaced with new patterns of positive behavior that will become superior habits.

Laszlo Bock is a senior vice president of People Operations at Google. He conducted a study of the company's best leaders. When you think of a leader, you typically picture someone who can rally the troops with a rousing speech or close a deal with a masterful script, but what the study found was that those were not the most important qualities for a leader.

What Google looks for in senior managers is predictability and consistency.

"For leaders, it's important for people to know that you are **consistent** and fair in how you think about making decisions and that there's an element of predictability. **If a leader is consistent, people on their teams experience tremendous freedom**, because then they know that within certain parameters, they can do whatever they want. If your manager is all over the place, you're never going to know what you can do, and you're going to experience it as very restrictive." (Emphasis added)

If, you want to read more, here is the link to an article about Google's take on leadership:
http://blog.idonethis.com/google-most-important-leadership-trait

Your consistent habits, which have become part of your behavior over time, have led you to your life and work realities. Whether you are fully aware of it, your habits are defining you and leading you every day. Ask yourself, are your habits leading you to where you want to go?

What are your thoughts on being defined as a person who leads your life with consistent behaviors?

_____

_____

_____

_____

_____

_____

Are there inconsistent behaviors that you would like to shift, change, dislodge or leave behind?

_____

_____

_____

Like competence, consistency is one of the three supports of our finished structure. Consistency affects your predictability and decreases uncertainty, which builds high levels of trust with others. Your ability to be reliable and stable absolutely matters!

CONSISTENCY
Be Prepared!

"Truth exists only as the individual himself produces it in action."
SØREN KIERKEGAARD

Everything you want in life requires focus on consistent training in mindset, talents, and skills. You understand the challenges of sustaining consistency as life constantly pulls you in a multitude of directions.

Take a moment to reflect on your current reality – What is your ability to perform all of your responsibilities?

Are you functioning at a high level every day? Be honest with yourself.

Where are you inconsistent? This reflection will help you to understand the areas in which you need to increase your consistency.

Life is full of opportunities to start ... and then stop. Every time you disconnect from one of your key responsibilities, you are creating an artificial roadblock to your progress.

Preparation for what you want in life and career happens when you consistently develop mindsets and good behaviors and implement them over a period of time.

Both your relationships and your career path, requires healthy beliefs, actions and emotionally intelligent preparation. Like almost everyone, you have doubtless had difficulty at times responding to new opportunities at work and in your personal lives, if you were not prepared. This is why we continue to emphasize, "Everything you want in life requires consistent training and focus."

It is likely that you find yourself setting a personal or professional goal, especially like most of us, during early January. You begin with enthusiasm and are willing to focus on your goal for a period of time. If you accomplish your goals quickly, great! But if you find yourself stuck or losing motivation while trying to accomplish those goals, it may mean that you need to develop new skills and apply them consistently in order to reach them. If you do not adjust the paradigm surrounding how you are trying to reach your goals and are not willing to develop new skills in order to reach them, you will find yourself in the same place as before, stuck again and even more frustrated and demotivated.

In order to achieve your desired goal, you must become a person who is consistently willing to do the effective steps needed to reach that goal.

We use the following messages when helping clients become the people they want to be and reach their personal and professional goals:

- When you are focused on being the person you want to be, you will train toward that end.
- When you are focused on what you need to do, you will look for ways to be equipped and increase in your skills.
- When you are willing and able to increase your capacity, you will develop and enhance your personal and professional skills, which will increase the probability of your new opportunities.

Preparation for what you want guides you to seeking new knowledge and builds your understanding of self-awareness. The reality of what you are capable of learning and implementing for your own development will be realized through your preparation. There are no shortcuts. Getting from where you are to where you want to go is a commitment to training and equipping yourself every day.

Dan Observes A Stunning Lack of Consistency

A few years back, I found it necessary to let one of my salespeople go. He was a very intelligent, "smart" guy, and I thought that he had all of the skills he needed to excel at the company.

From the beginning, he was consistently trained in the company's processes for new employees. I was hopeful and excited about his future success.

Two months later, this new hire was failing miserably. It became clear that he chose not to take any of the training seriously. Sometimes, the trouble with "smart" people is that they think they have a better way to do something than what has proved successful. I didn't anticipate his reluctance to follow the sales process. Subsequently, he failed to approach customers with any of the consistent behaviors that were built into that process.

Upon seeing his initial lack of results, I coached him in the areas that needed improvement. Unfortunately, he continued his behavior and refused to prepare for his customer calls. Even though he had been provided with a proven and effective blueprint for success, rather than consistently and faithfully following the plan, instead he consistently failed in performing the necessary prep work to set himself up for success.

Eventually, the inevitable end arrived, and we parted ways. I learned a valuable lesson in managing people: When leading, training, and preparing people to be consistent in their approach to work for greater success, I found that if they refuse to listen to my expertise the first time, I had to learn that they were not going to listen to my expertise the second, third, or, God forbid, the fourth time around!

Tess Observes Consistency at Home

A couple of years ago, my husband, Dean, decided to train for his first 5K run. As he researched different training methods, he chose the "Couch-to-5K" method. His focus was to train, equip himself to run, and increase his odds of completing the run without feeling miserable or regretting the endeavor.

He trained with the realization that it would take his body time to respond to his new habit of running. The running, jogging, walking, and day-off routine equipped him for his first race. There was no pressure, no one was keeping track of his progress, and he was not accountable to anyone except himself.

Two months later, he ran his first 5K. As he crossed the finish line he had a great feeling of accomplishment. Two years later, he was consistently participating in 5K's and half marathons. His one full marathon may be his only one, yet he continues to keep himself in shape with running and training. Now he has people who like to run with him because he is so consistent. He was consistent in developing and maintaining the following:

- A paradigm shift
- A new goal
- A new set of behaviors and habits
- A new way to practice, train, and equip himself
- A new outcome of success!

Tess Coaches A Leader to Build an Agenda

One of my clients chose "preparing for meetings" as one of his coaching goals. This client is a senior vice president and a very capable, intelligent, and skilled individual. One of his personality traits is to rise to the occasion when under pressure. He is at his most creative when feeling a sense of urgency. He is very competent and has the ability to draw from his vast knowledge and years of experience in his industry.

With new owners and a new CEO at the helm of his business, he found his leadership in meetings suffered from a lack of preparation. He needed to act quickly and change his behavior, which had been sufficient in the past. His old behaviors were not going to work in this new reality.

One of the steps I used to help him be better prepared, was the creation of a simple agenda and his decision to actually follow it. He began to use consistent methods of behavior and clear forms of dialogue within the context of meetings. He was more concise and focused on what others needed to know and hear.

The noticeable positive results and outcomes came with affirmation from his boss and peers. They began to show their appreciation for the work he was doing and how he was leading. Trust was built because of his capacity to communicate consistently with greater clarity and understanding. His ability to become a vital member of the team in the company's progress with its strategy and plans was further established and enforced with his change of behavior.

<u>What are three productive habits that will train, equip, and prepare you for greater consistency?</u>

1) _____

_____

2) _____

_____

3) _____

_____

What are you willing to do or sacrifice to increase your capacity to prepare so that you can become more consistent?

_____

_____

_____

List three key things you've learned about consistency:

1) _____
   _____
   _____
   _____

2) _____
   _____
   _____
   _____

3) _____
   _____
   _____
   _____

Reflect and focus on your consistency:

What would happen to your life, career, and relationships if you increased and transformed your ability to be consistent?

_____
_____

What problem(s) in your life, career, and relationships would be solved if you focused on and increased your ability to be consistent?

_____
_____

In the areas of training, equipping yourself with new tools and preparing for what you want, what do you need to change to become more consistent?

_____
_____

CONSISTENCY
Be Prepared!

You are what you train to be.
    Today – Focus on being ready:
    <u>**Be consistent in the following:**</u>

- **Training to be the person you want to be**
  Determine the training that will help you.

- **Equipping and preparing yourself**
  Determine your present abilities and establish what tools will help you to move from where you are to where you want to be.

<u>**Read the above at least three times today.**</u>
What do the statements mean to you?

_____

_____

How will you incorporate their meaning into your daily interactions with others?

_____

<u>**Take the temperature of your CONSISTENCY:**</u>
On a scale of 1-5 (1 being low and 5 being high), assess the quality of your consistency in work.

_____

On a scale of 1-5 (1 being low and 5 being high), assess the quality of your consistency in your relationships.

_____

WEEK 1 / THURSDAY

CREATIVITY
Pillar Number 3

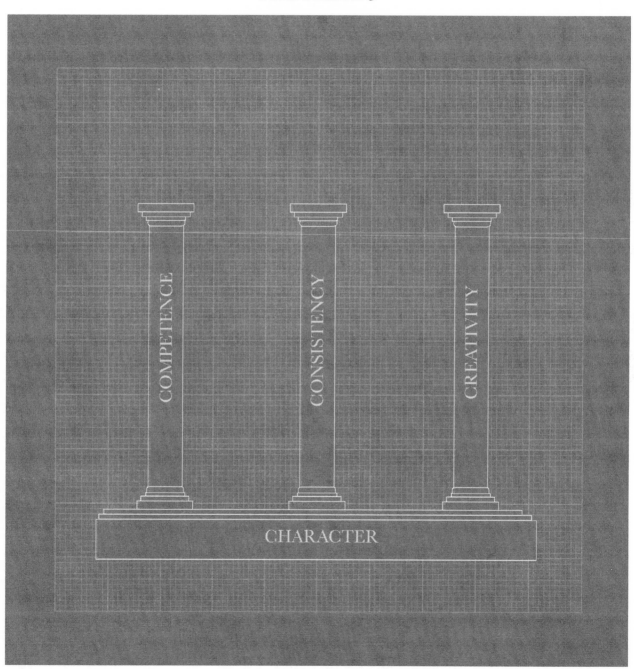

An influential person has the ability to create strong relationships and build trust with others. They are able to think of new ideas and process input with others. Their solutions produce excellent outcomes for the good of themselves and others.

> **"Creativity requires faith.**
> **Faith requires that we relinquish control."**
> JULIA CAMERON
> AUTHOR, PLAYWRIGHT, SONGWRITER AND POET

Creativity is the third and final support to our structure. Creativity is the art of looking at things in new or different ways, and as a result bringing something new into reality. With technology a part of our everyday lives, we live in increasingly creative times. Technology has infused the world with a host of unique ways to create, communicate, and do things differently. It has given us the opportunity to accomplish things on our own that were previously considered impossible. The effects of creativity in our lives are never-ending.

What goes through your mind when you think of the word "creativity"? Do you think of an artist, musician, or writer? It is possible; you do not see yourself as a person with artistic abilities.

Yet, every day you lead yourself, participate in relationships, perform tasks, hone your skills, and use your intellect. At the end of each day, on some level, you have creatively navigated your way through a number of relationships and responsibilities. Creativity is part of the structural philosophy of our leadership blueprint. Leading your own personal and professional life is an art, and being responsible for others in work and life involves more creativity than you might think.

As we focus on creativity, our intent is to support you to think more conceptually – imagining new ideas or ways of doing things. Your personality type may like to gather information with facts and data, so envisioning new ideas may not be the way you consider making changes. If this is true for you, it will be helpful for you to surround yourself with people who think in a more abstract or theoretical way. That said, part of growth and development is to see things differently. Practicing creativity gives you an opportunity to shape a new way of seeing, thinking and being in all aspects of your life and work.

Creativity comes in many forms, and it may take courage to explore and discover creativity within and by you.

We're going to ask you to:

- Embrace change
- Become curious
- Overcome obstacles
- Develop a vision for yourself

Don't worry – we will not be asking you to draw or paint a picture. We will not be asking you to write a book, an article, or a blog. Although, if you are gifted in any of these areas, please feel free to do so.

Take it past your limits when it comes to implementing new creativity and let yourself be open to new ways of thinking creatively.

> **"To live in a great idea is to treat the impossible as though it were possible."**
> JOHANN WOLFGANG VON GOETHE

Your ability to learn and listen to your inner creativity will propel you to greater heights. The key is to be true to your inner self and create what is important to you.

Creativity Blossoms

An artist friend of Tess' never knew she had artistic ability until she was well into her thirties. When her children were little, she began to draw, paint, and decorate – a new passion had emerged within her, and a new talent was discovered that she had not known existed until that point in time. She has gone on to build a viable business that allows others to enjoy her creativity. She paints and creates home décor pieces and sells her merchandise online and to national retailers.

There are times when creativity can help both sides get what they want. In business, one of the greatest places to find creativity is in negotiations. Surely, you have heard the story of the sisters who are fighting over an orange. They both wanted the orange for themselves and would stop at nothing to get it. They were headed for a true win/lose situation, until their mother suggested they find out "why" each wanted the orange. As it turns out, one needed the flesh to make juice and the other needed the rind to make a pie. Finding out what each other wanted, they were able to both attain the piece of the orange they wanted.

The creative desire moves every entrepreneur forward to create a business plan, search for investors, create an executive team, set the vision, and address reality. Those who see new possibilities for the future that others do not see are living creatively.

Richard Branson launched Virgin Records in 1973. Today, the Virgin Group holds more than 200 companies in more than 30 countries.

Born on July 18, 1950, in Surrey, England, Branson struggled in school and dropped out at age 16. He began a magazine called, *Student* that was focused on the youth culture. *Student* was for the students and run by the students. As the magazine needed capital, Branson's creativity expanded with the idea to begin a mail-order record company. He called it *Virgin*, which ultimately led to the creation of *Virgin Records*. His entrepreneurial projects started in the music industry and expanded into other sectors, making Branson a billionaire. His *Virgin Group* spans multiple industries including music, airlines, and even *Virgin Galactic*, a space-tourism company. Branson is also known for his adventurous spirit and sporting achievements, including crossing oceans in a hot air balloon.

You may not be a Richard Branson. Yet, creativity exists within you. If you work to release it, your creativity will manifest itself uniquely in you. You have the choice of whether to silence or ignore it. Creativity is always with you, seeking to be acknowledged and brought into existence.

Think about your creative focus. Has creativity developed and grown in your life? How?

_____

_____

_____

Tess Discovers Her Own Unique Way Of Creativity

I began to understand a different and creative side of me as I worked with people unlike me – people with varying historical and family backgrounds, education, personality types, life experiences, career choices and talents. I found (and still find) my client's and their stories fascinating.

My expertise has helped people develop an understanding of their own stories through learning, growing, and embracing change within themselves. Every person I work with requires a unique coaching approach and listening skills. This solid pillar of creativity has brought consistently successful results as I enter into the lives of others and navigate through a wide variety of complex stories and personalities. Creativity, my willingness to keep an open mind, discern without judgment and ask good questions has allowed me to build long-lasting relationships with my clients as well.

Every client is a unique individual with their own strengths, gaps, opportunities, and challenges to creating the life they want to live. With each client, I need to creatively use different styles of communication in order to coach them effectively.

For some, a straightforward and very clear approach is required to help them build better understanding and self-awareness. Others need words of encouragement and support pertaining to their circumstances and what they are seeking to accomplish.

What I find fascinating is the opportunity to create a unique dialogue with each client during my day and communicate in the specific style that each client needs. I may not be "creating" like my artist friend, or like Richard Branson, but I am rewarded by living creatively every day via my communication with my clients, family, friends, and colleagues.

Creativity requires thought, process, and the willingness (courage) to try something new.

> **"If a man does not keep pace with his companions,**
> **perhaps it is because he hears a different drummer.**
> **Let him step to the music which he hears,**
> **however measured or far away."**
> HENRY DAVID THOREAU

CREATIVITY
Embrace Healthy Change

**"Leaders take charge of change.
They instill a sense of adventure in others,
they look for ways to radically alter the status quo,
and they continuously scan the outside environment
for new and fresh ideas. Leaders always search for
opportunities and for ways to do what has never been done."**
JAMES KOUZES AND BARRY POSNER
"THE LEADERSHIP CHALLENGE:
HOW TO MAKE EXTRAORDINARY THINGS HAPPEN IN ORGANIZATIONS"

To grow and develop as a leader requires you to change who you are on some level. We are not talking about changing 180 degrees from who you are just for the sake of change. This will not serve you well.

We are talking about you imagining how to get from the reality of where you are today, to the vision of where you want to be. You will be using what works well for you and changing what doesn't, so you can begin to live a life that is meaningful to you. It will require you to begin a process of personal change in how you manage your own self; in order to create the change you need, for you to move forward and toward who you want to be.

You may be fearful about change because you have not yet discovered its positive and healthy benefits. It can be hard to envision change, so sticking with the familiar seems the only logical choice. We understand there is overwhelming comfort in the familiar.

You may be reluctant to embrace change because of one major issue: You always seem to find yourself doing what you already know how to do. Over the years, your behaviors have been repeated countless times and they have become your norm of doing what you know to do.

When you really want to change for the better and are ready for change, what needs to happen, both for you and for others?

In order to effect real change, you will have to make a personal choice to look at your deepest motives.

Personal change is more difficult to embrace when you have already established yourself with education and expertise. Who wants to go back to being or feeling like a beginner and the insecure feeling that comes with learning something new?

Within the last several years, changes in our economy have required many people to change where they live, where they work, and even their expectations about the American dream. In some cases, those outside forces have even caused change in their relationships.

Those who sought healthy change chose to use these economic challenges as an opportunity to face fears and create new lives for themselves and their families. Many new jobs, and even industries, were created during this difficult economic time.

Crisis sometimes forces change upon us. Fear of the unknown or the inability to touch or feel the change that is needed, along with the fear of your ability to work through change, is extremely challenging. But the results of change are this: When you let go of what is not working and embrace something new that will work to your advantage, *life gets better*.

When deciding to make a change, we suggest baby steps, what we like to call incremental change. Don't try to change 180 degrees, swinging the pendulum and going in the opposite direction (like attempting a marathon without first training for a 5K). At its best, change is a process that takes time to unfold. This makes change become attainable rather than untenable. A measured rate of change increases the likelihood that your new habit or your new way of being will stick. When seeking to make a change, time is on your side.

Remember the examples of the British cycling team and Dean's running his first 5K? It's all about the consistent practice of a new habit.

Don't be concerned about the distance you think you need to go. Change is only one small choice away every single day.

Helpful reminders when developing and trying something new:

- Suspend judgment.
- Give yourself permission to fail.
- If you fall, get back up and keep moving.
- A step back isn't the end of the road.
- Ask others for help, support or advice.

What A Client Thinks They Want

Dan: When we first meet prospective clients, we will sometimes ask, "What is your comfort level and tolerance for change?" The higher their tolerance for change, the greater our ability to serve them with new ideas.

It's interesting to observe prospective clients. The companies we call on tend to believe they want improvement. They tell us they want to do things better and more efficiently. Yet, my salespeople experience a resistance to change every day because of the prospects' fear of it and because of one of the most powerful forces on earth: the status quo.

We do not ask our clients to embrace change that will impact the fundamental truths and values by which they live and work. We communicate to our clients: "If you are looking for new and better ways to do, say, and think about the things you already hold dear, we can help you discover and develop what will work best for you, which will deliver different results for your organization."

Those clients who are willing to change and develop a more streamlined operation (often needed in most industries) subsequently experience an advantage over their competitors. The new truth: The old way of doing things is no longer working, and a new way of doing things will increase your productivity and improve your life.

One caveat: Some people embrace constant change, never sticking with anything long enough to master it and experience results. They are continuously on the move and tend to move so fast from one thing to the next that they become frenetic and not very productive or effective. This is not what we are promoting when considering embracing change.

"Somewhere along the line of development we discover what we really are,
and then we make our real decision for which we are responsible.
Make that decision primarily for yourself because you can never
really have anyone else's life, not even your own child's.
The influence you have is through your own life
and what you become yourself."

ELEANOR ROOSEVELT

Write your personal / professional change story:

_____
_____
_____
_____
_____
_____
_____
_____
_____
_____
_____
_____
_____
_____
_____
_____
_____
_____
_____
_____
_____

<u>List three key things you've learned about creativity:</u>

1) _____
_____
_____

2) _____
_____
_____

3) _____
_____
_____

Reflect and focus on your creativity:

What would happen to your life, career, and relationships if you increased, changed, or transformed your ability to be more creative?

_____

_____

What problems in your life, career, and relationships would be solved if you focused on and increased your comfort level with being more creative?

_____

_____

In the areas of keeping an open mind, having a favorable attitude, and being engaged with transformational change, what do you need to change to become more creative?

_____

_____

❖ ❖ ❖

CREATIVITY
Embrace Healthy Change

You are what you create.
    Today – Focus on making a difference by bringing:

- An open mind when adopting something new
- A favorable attitude when experiencing change and trying something new
- A level of self-awareness to personally grow and develop for transformational change

<u>Read the above at least three times today.</u>
What do the statements mean to you?

_____

_____

How will you incorporate their meaning into your daily interactions with others?

_____

<u>Take the temperature of your CREATIVITY:</u>
On a scale of 1-5 (1 being low and 5 being high), assess the present quality of your creativity at work.

_____

On a scale of 1-5 (1 being low and 5 being high), assess the present quality of your creativity in your relationships.

_____

<u>WEEK 1 / FRIDAY</u>

CONFIDENCE
The Protective Cover

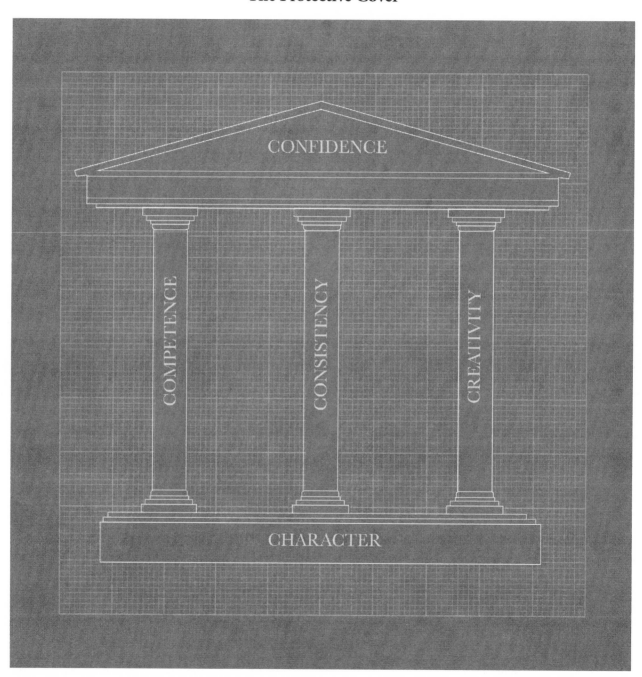

A person who possesses confidence personally and professionally builds trust with others. The quality of their communication is high, and they excel when resolving conflicts. They are able to influence others through listening, gathering feedback, and collaborating with others to find solutions for best results. Confidence is fully realized through the development of the first four C's.

> **"A confident leader is one who is able to**
> **celebrate the wins of others,**
> **compete with good intent,**
> **have courageous dialogue to enhance relationships**
> **and stay resilient during challenging times."**
> Tess Cox

Confidence. You may be very self-assured and capable in your roles and responsibilities at home and work. Or, you may be a person who finds confidence to be a constant challenge.

How does one attain confidence?

_____

_____

What do confident people look like or do?

_____

_____

There can be confident people in any profession and walk of life, regardless of their socioeconomic condition.

Confidence is a natural byproduct of living well in the previous areas we've covered. Check the areas where you are most confident:

_____You are the authority over your own character.

_____You have attained a level of personal and professional competence.

_____You are consistent, expressing what you need and receiving what you want when building relationships that are important to you.

_____You understand all of life needs to be creative, whether relating with one person or many people. Your individual expression is communicated in all that you do and say.

_____You know what you believe and value. You have a personal philosophy.

_____You think for yourself and are able to share your thoughts and opinions with others.

_____You appreciate and value recognition, but do not rely on the approval of others to derive self-worth.

_____You are able to influence the behaviors and opinions of others.

_____You are able to lead yourself and others well.

_____You are confident in who you are – willing to adjust your approach when living and working with others.

_____You are confident, able to lead your life effectively and live meaningfully.

Confidence cannot be purchased, loaned, or sold. Confidence is an accumulation of good, healthy, and challenging experiences.

Being who you are and knowing why you do things impacts all of your outcomes.

All of your confident choices matter!

CONFIDENCE
Self-Awareness

A Review of Your Learning:
Reflect on how you have become more self-aware in the areas mentioned above. Write your thoughts below:

- **Integrity – Character**

  _____

  _____

  _____

  _____

- **Learning – Competence**

  _____

  _____

  _____

  _____

- **Preparation – Consistency**

  _____

  _____

  _____

  _____

- **Embracing change – Creativity**

  _____

  _____

  _____

  _____

Reflect and focus on your Confidence:
What would happen to your life, career, and relationships if you increased or transformed your ability to be more confident?

_____

_____

What problems in your life, career, and relationships would be solved if you focused on and changed your confidence?

_____

_____

In the areas of building trust with others, learning, unlearning, and reshaping your paradigms, being prepared and embracing good and healthy change, what do you need to change to become more confident?

Dan: A Story of Confidence

I began selling for a living in 2001 when I became a Realtor at the age of 20. At an early age, I liked to promote and persuade others with my enthusiasm. It seemed like a natural fit to go into a career of selling real estate, which played to my strengths.

The problem was, I wasn't really a "capable" salesperson. I had enthusiasm and not much else. When I found myself in difficult situations, I would feel a strong sense of internal panic. If you've spent any time in sales, you know this is not a winning feeling. Even if I could occasionally mask my unease, it didn't make the job enjoyable. My results were certainly not as good as they could have been if I had been a confident and capable professional.

Here is my key understanding of what went wrong for me in real estate: I could not effectively sell if I did not believe in the product. As a Realtor, the product was me and my ability to get a home sold.

Looking back, I have to laugh at my blind ambition, because today I can tell you, for SURE, that I would not have put something as important as the sale of my home in the hands of a 20 year-old young man who could barely shave. The truth is, I did sell eight houses in my first year. But the fact was, I didn't truly enjoy it, nor did I have the confidence to build out my career in home sales for sustainability.

Now, let me fast-forward sixteen years. I now lead a team of seven high-powered salespeople who come to me regularly for advice on creating a strong strategy in complicated sales situations.

At this point in my career, I am completely at ease in just about every selling situation I and my team find ourselves in. I truly believe that my company and I represent the best opportunities for our prospects and customers. Simply stated, I know our company can realize the best possible outcomes for our customers and their businesses.

What changed during those sixteen years?

- I've made more than 25,000 sales calls. I left real estate in 2008 and became a corporate sales representative for an industrial packaging company. I was required to make more than twenty physical face-to-face sales calls every day. I have continued this commitment to my organizations and myself for over the last eight years.
- While following the requirements and processes of the company, I fell down, picked myself up, adjusted my approach, and kept making the calls on many days when I didn't feel like doing it.
- I learned to adapt my approach over time. I've changed and refined the words I use and how I say them. While my approach used to be to ask something like, "Is Mark available?" I now approach and warmly greet a gatekeeper, stating, "I'm here to see Mark." This subtle shift in words has increased my success rate and ability to move ahead to the next step of the sales process.
- I've learned to change the questions I ask and the order in which I ask them.

- In situations where I used to offer to save people money, I now ask questions about their business and processes to determine if saving money is even possible.
- One thing I didn't change was the consistency of my actions. Consistency was the hallmark of these sales calls. I would visit customers every two weeks. That consistency allowed me to learn fast as I became more competent, and it allowed me to build trust with my customers.
- I have attended more than thirty live seminars that cover selling, sales management, and personal development.
- I have supplemented those seminars with hundreds of hours of YouTube videos as I watch other seminars. Many seminars given ten to twenty years ago by brilliant people still hold up today.
- I've built a library of and read, more than 300 books to further my personal development. These book topics include how to talk to people, reading body language, psychology, influence, marketing, presenting, and leading teams. All of my learning fuels my creativity, which in turn gives me the confidence to test new things and add new pieces to my sales process.

You could view this as a ton of work, but it has never felt like it because I am passionate about all of these topics. I have found that the more I read, study, and adjust my approach, the more skilled and confident I become. As I practice and become better at my sales craft, the more fun selling is. As we enter a customer's place of business, my sales team is full of positive energy. It's my goal to make my team's sales calls the best thing that happens in the customer's building that day … and we are succeeding.

As you learn what is important to you, true confidence takes shape in your life. As you understand your strengths and qualities and put good strategies into practice, you too, can become a force to be reckoned with.

Let me encourage you, if you aren't feeling confident today, start down the path of learning, implement what you learn, and stay with it … because the road to getting where you want to be is worth it.

"Trust yourself.
Create the kind of self
that you will be happy to live with all your life.
Make the most of yourself by fanning the tiny,
inner sparks of possibility into flames of achievement."
GOLDA MEIR

CONFIDENCE
Self-Awareness

Today – Focus on the past four days as you reflect on the following:

- **Character**
  Building trust with others – being a person of integrity.

- **Competence**
  Learning – unlearning and reshaping who you are and how you do things.

- **Consistency**
  Being prepared.

- **Creativity**
  Embracing good and healthy change.

These four areas will build your self-awareness and confidence in who you are personally and professionally and why you do what you do in life and work.

<u>Read the above at least three times today.</u>
What do the statements mean to you?

_____

_____

How will you incorporate their meaning into your daily interactions with others?

_____

<u>Take the temperature of your confidence:</u>
On a scale of 1-5 (1 being low and 5 being high), assess the present quality of your confidence at work.

_____

On a scale of 1-5 (1 being low and 5 being high), assess the present quality of your confidence in your relationships.

_____

WEEK 2 / MONDAY

CHARACTER
Be Incredible – Raise the Bar for Yourself

A person of character knows who they are and why they do what they do. They are able to build trust with others through their integrity, trustworthiness, and honesty.

In his leadership fable, "The Five Dysfunctions of A Team," Patrick Lencioni talks about a CEO facing the ultimate leadership crisis. The "team" had more "experienced and talented executives than its competitors. It had more cash and better technology than its competitors. It had a more powerful board of directors." Yet, in spite of all it had going for it, the team was "behind two of their competitors in terms of both revenue and customer growth."

How could this be possible? Throughout the book, Lencioni describes how the executives were caught in the grip of dysfunction – a lack of character, competence, consistency, creativity and confidence. The bar of excellence had progressively declined so low that the board decided to hire an outside person as CEO to raise that bar before the team could begin to live up to its potential.

See if you can relate to any of these dysfunctions of character in your own life or work:

- No trust
- Inability to address conflict
- No commitment
- No accountability
- No results

The moral of this story is, you can have experience, talent, expertise, and money, and yet, if you do not continue to "raise the bar" for yourself and others, at some point, your success peaks and is not sustainable, and a downward trend ensues.

Think about the character of your leadership. How will you fill in your blanks?

"I have more _____ and _____ than those I work with. I have more _____ and _____ than others. I have more _____. Yet, in spite of all that I have going for me, I am still behind in _____."

Are you familiar with the Sigmoid Curve?

The Sigmoid Curve represents the philosophy of being "incredible" (doing more than you think is possible) and "raising the bar" (making something larger or greater) for yourself and others. Every new venture begins with an idea, which goes through a birthing process. This is when much of the hard work is done.

Once the idea, goal, or business plan is in place, it gathers momentum through strategies that are planned and executed. This momentum creates new levels of success. With that new success, a sense of relief is experienced because of all of the consistent focus and hard work has paid off.

The danger in this process is that some leaders and employees are susceptible to resting on their past successes and neglect to start a new creative process. Entropy ensues, and the curve turns downward and begins to decline because leaders and employees are too busy managing their own past success.

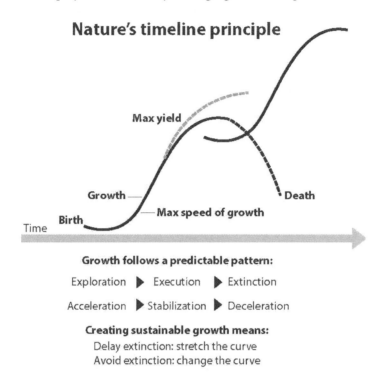

Nature's timeline principle

Max yield

Growth —

Max speed of growth

Birth

Death

Time

Growth follows a predictable pattern:

Exploration ▶ Execution ▶ Extinction

Acceleration ▶ Stabilization ▶ Deceleration

Creating sustainable growth means:
Delay extinction: stretch the curve
Avoid extinction: change the curve

You've probably heard the story of the frog sitting in a pot of lukewarm water on a slowly warming stove. As the water continues to warm, the frog does not notice the increasing heat until it is much too late to jump out of the boiling water. The frog is doomed!

The slow death of an idea, venture or organization is subtle, and you rarely see the signs until it is too late to do anything about the pending failure. Consistently, staying true to building trust, addressing conflict, being committed and accountable, leads you to launching new ideas and processes. Your character is critical to your results and sustaining meaningful personal and professional growth.

In order to be "incredible" (doing more than you think is possible) and "raising the bar" (making something larger or greater) for yourself and others, which is building your character, you must be intentional about:

- Why you do things
- How you do things
- What things you need to do

In his book "Standout," Marcus Buckingham tells the story of Ralph, a Best Buy electronics store manager:

"Ralph had successfully transformed one of Best Buy's lowest-performing stores into a repeat award winner." Buckingham wanted to know how Ralph took his team from "the bottom 10 percent to the top."

As told to him by Ralph, Buckingham explains: "Since initially his store was at the bottom of every district performance table, he wanted to give his people a way to celebrate that **excellence was indeed happening** in his store, and that **it was happening all the time.** So he gave everyone a whistle and told (his employees) to blow the whistle whenever they saw anyone do anything good. It didn't matter if the person they saw was their superior or was working over in another department; if they saw somebody **go above and beyond**, they were to blow the whistle." Buckingham wondered "if this tactic had made the store incredibly loud." (Emphasis added)

Ralph's response was, "Sure, but it energized the store. It energized me. Heck, it even energized the customers. They loved it."

This story reminds us of the power of our own energy when we know that we are being incredible and raising the bar for others and ourselves. When you have this kind of energy, others want to be around you and will follow you. In a symbolic way others are blowing their whistles because they see you performing to a higher standard, going above and beyond what is asked of you, doing more for others, and having a vision about future possibilities.

Energy is a capacity for performing work. It propels you to do something. It helps you to develop new ideas and revise existing ideas. Remember the Sigmoid Curve? Energy gives you the ability to focus your behaviors as you work above and beyond minimum expectations, continue to seek excellence and help you sustain growth. Building your character is not satisfied with the status quo of who you are and how you do things.

You may wonder, "How does the sigmoid curve and energy have anything to do with character?" Growth is an essential function of your character. As the leader of yourself, the ability to focus on where you invest your energy for personal growth will lead you to create the direction you want to go. Your character is energy and it will influence your outcomes when it lives fully.

Character Displayed in the Sales Arena

The salespeople on Dan's team sell against competitors with varying levels of skill. This could create a problem if we weren't committed to excellence, the foundation of character.

In every situation in which more than one salesperson is calling on a customer, there exists a phenomenon I call value disparity – a noticeable difference in the quality and value of the salespeople. The disparity creates a situation in which the "lower value" salesperson unwittingly promotes the "higher value" salesperson.

To illustrate how this works, look at two salespeople:

Jim shows up at an account in a random fashion, never on the same day of the week, usually at different times of the day. He'll run over at the drop of a hat when the customer calls. This limits his calls to three or four, per day depending on what develops. He usually wears a polo shirt and jeans, and his usual approach is to stop in and say any number of low-value, self-centered things:

"What's going on?"

"Do you have anything for me?"

"Can I work on something for you?"

"I'd love an opportunity!"

"I was just in the area."

Jim may have a foundation of character when building his relationships with his customers and yet, all of the above comments and actions equate to "no" energy and influence. He is choosing to live and work with a status quo mindset, which will move him to a certain point in his life and work, but it will not move him towards further growth and development.

Meanwhile, Tim begins calling on the same account every other Monday at 10:00 a.m. He's dressed in a shirt and tie and dress slacks, and he always brings something interesting or useful to show the customer.

He asks questions that help him gain insight into the buyer's life and company.

He builds a relationship with the buyer.

He presents the item he brought to share in a compelling fashion.

All of the above actions equate to "high" energy and influence.

Tim's character and mindset are focused on what value and contributions he can bring to his buyer.

Regardless of who may be the incumbent vendor today, who do you think is more likely to own the account a year from now?

Tim's valuable, energy-filled and consistent approach is stellar. He leaves nothing to chance; his wardrobe, work habits, and relationship building are all careful, considered choices based on his character – who he is, which influences his outcomes.

This creates an incredible gap of value between the two salespeople. Doesn't Jim's lackadaisical, low-energy approach make Tim look amazing in comparison? Jim likely has no idea about the noticeable value disparity and its effect of amplifying Tim's value. He fails to realize nothing exists in a vacuum. Likewise, Tim is making Jim look absolutely terrible, whereas, without comparison with Tim, Jim may have otherwise seemed just "OK" in the eyes of the buyer.

Would you rather be viewed as a Jim or a Tim?

This example represents two character choices, which over time will lead you down two potential paths:

- A compounding return of excellence with energy and influence with others. You stand out.
  or
- Endless mediocrity with no energy or interest from others. You blend in with everyone else.

Raise the bar – go above and beyond in your tasks at work and home – and you will be noticed, appreciated, and valued.

Wherever you are, someone is watching you either go above and beyond or do just enough to get by. Regardless of what your professional or financial incentives are, do the right things and deliver the best results. Over time, your rewards will go above and beyond what you thought was possible because growth produces energy, and energy creates momentum, and momentum creates an incredible flow of forward movement.

**"We are what we repeatedly do.
Excellence is not an act, but a habit."**
ARISTOTLE

Think about your own "raise the bar" moments, when you knew you were working at your highest level of excellence. Note three key behaviors you exhibited at the time.

1) _____

_____

2) _____

_____

3) _____

_____

Now, think about the power of your own character. Are others drawn to your desire to create, grow and move yourself forward with energy that influences others?

_____

_____

_____

_____

Ask yourself the following questions:

- Have I bought the lie, "This is how it's always going to be"?
- Am I doing what I thought three years ago I would be doing now?
- Have I accepted "good enough" as my best outcome?

Note your thoughts on these questions.

_____

_____

_____

_____

_____

_____

_____

Entrepreneur Jim Rohn said, "If a man says, 'I'm making about $50,000 a year! Isn't that good enough?' Yes, that's good enough, if that's all you're capable of doing. If that's your full potential, then that's great. However, if you make $50,000, but you're capable of making $500,000, then we would call you somewhat of a loser.

It's not about the money, it's about realizing the full potential of your reach and influence."

Are you living at the full level of your potential?

_____

_____

_____

If you are on the right track, great.
If you need more support to get back on track, that's what we're here for.

Keep reading, learning, and growing.
We believe you can be incredible.

CHARACTER
Be Incredible – Raise the Bar for Yourself

Today – Focus on finding a higher standard of excellence in the following ways:

- Go above and beyond in your tasks at work and home
- Think of new possibilities for yourself and how to do them
- Simply have the mindset - choose to be amazing, not just for one day, but every day!

<u>Read the above at least three times today.</u>
What do the statements mean to you?

_____

_____

How will you incorporate their meaning into your daily interactions with others?

_____

WEEK 2 / TUESDAY

COMPETENCE
Communicate with your highest level of clarity

A person of competence understands the reality of their skills and knows how they bring value to their relationships and work with their expertise. They are able to build trust with others through their well-known capabilities, qualifications, and experiences.

> **"We must take care not to make the intellect our god.**
> **It has, of course, powerful muscles,**
> **but no personality.**
> **It cannot lead, it can only serve."**
> ALBERT EINSTEIN

Intellect alone will not build relationships or create effective leadership. We have found the most often desired leadership traits are intellect and skills. While these two areas of who you are and how you do things are important, building strong and healthy relationships is far more important.

Here's something to think about: It doesn't do you any good to be the smartest person in the room if no one wants to be in the room with you.

What does Einstein's quote mean to you?

_____

_____

_____

_____

One way to build creative leadership and strong relationships is through clear, intentional communication. By self-managing your communication, you understand your internal thoughts before you speak and while you are forming thoughts verbally. A dialogue that is transparent, clear with intent, and includes a willingness to listen to others will create a strong sense of trust in all of your relationships.

Can you think of a time when you stopped yourself and internally said, "I shouldn't say that!"? Or, "I shouldn't go there!" Note your experience(s) below:

_____

_____

_____

_____

We (Dan and Tess) have high word quotients when communicating with others, and we experience a need to self-manage our own thoughts and words before we speak them. We understand it is extremely difficult to communicate effectively when our emotions are high and when we are not in agreement with another person. During these times, using self-management behaviors, we seek to listen to our inner selves, slow our emotional impulses down, pause before responding, mirror what the other person is saying, and attempt to communicate appropriately and wisely. Is this difficult…YES! Yet, the more we practice our inner thinking and self-manage our outward behaviors, the more skilled we become at communicating clearly with our best intent.

Jack Canfield writes in his book "The Success Principles" that being a conscious master of your own words creates greater success when you "speak words that will build self-esteem and self-confidence, build relationships, and build dreams – words of affirmation, encouragement, appreciation, love, acceptance, possibility, and vision." Communication is powerful. Your words matter, and they have power!

Dan has a weekly meeting with his sales team. They study two things: product knowledge and sales skills. They schedule this time together so they can be a team of competent, knowledgeable salespeople.

The company can't have packaging geniuses who do not know how to communicate, sell, and build relationships with their clients. The salespeople and the company would never see positive results.

Likewise, it would be futile to have a crop of great communicators who can make great connections with potential clients but know nothing about the facts and details of the products they are selling. They would lose credibility immediately.

There are two types of competence: a technical aptitude with the ability to gain knowledge that relates to your specific job, and relational abilities that apply to interacting with others. Competence in emotional intelligence is to understand your emotions and notice when strong emotions emerge within you. When you are able to harness your own emotions and connect with others, you are able to manage your relationships well. Managing yourself within the context of being in relationship with others, is one of the most powerful forms of competence, affecting everything in your life on every level.

Write the name of someone who makes you feel better when you are with them.

_____

Write the name of a person who makes you laugh.

_____

Write the name of a person you can't wait to see again.

_____

Write the name of a person who tells wonderful stories.

_____

Thinking about the qualities of these individuals will help you realize why you respond to them in a positive way. You may value their unique style, their ability to listen, or their expertise in communicating with you and others. You may like being with them because they make you feel good and set an encouraging tone for you and others.

You experience a true sense of meaning when you are with others whose thoughts and views you respect and appreciate. You enjoy hearing what they have to say, and feel a sense of gratitude when they include and help you belong. This is why social media is so popular. You are interested in what certain people have to say and the ways in which they say it, so much so that you are willing to "follow" them because they make you feel like you are a part of their world and influence.

"Successful people are the master of their words."
Jack Canfield
AUTHOR OF THE "CHICKEN SOUP FOR THE SOUL" SERIES

A High-Stakes Meeting

In the spring of 2012, Tess was in Singapore training a diverse team. The team consisted of sales, customer service, finance, IT, and HR professionals from all over the Asia Pacific region. Back in New York, the corporate office had an extremely high expectation of this team's ability to work together and perform at the top level for its shareholders.

Significant financial goals had been set, and the board, company worldwide sales teams, and stakeholders were watching. These professionals were well trained, knowledgeable, and experts in their field. The problem: They lacked the ability to listen to one another and collaborate as a team. Understandably, it was challenging because they were working remotely in different parts of a vast region. Was it even possible for this team to work together?

Tess found that they did not have a basic foundation of knowledge about one another that would help them create the dialogue of shared meaning that would lead to a strategy of success. With Tess' help and support, the team's job was to create enough trust and accountability to allow this diverse group of individuals to work together as a team to reach the desired, and highly anticipated results.

After two days of focused and intense training, which built around listening to one another, addressing the issues at hand, honestly valuing the expertise and commitment of one another, and creating strategies for results, the CEO of the company spoke to the team via videoconference from New York City.

He reiterated the expectation that the company was relying on them to perform at its highest level. The stakes were high, and the call to action was intentional, direct, and powerful. Every word he spoke was chosen with precise purpose. He communicated to all that he was certain they could reach the goals set before them by the executive team.

Why could they reach the goals? The CEO recognized their combined intellectual knowledge, their accumulative professional experience, and their individual expertise that created not just a good team, but also a great team!

The CEO knew every team member was capable of reaching the required goals. Would it be difficult? Yes. Yet, if they implemented collaborative efforts – listening to one another, respecting the differences between each other and communicating effectively – they would not only reach the desired goals, but they also had the potential to go above and beyond them.

In closing, the CEO exhorted them to keep clear lines of consistent communication and an ongoing dialogue, which would keep everyone committed and accountable to the goals. Lastly, he challenged the team to get ready. Get ready to rise to the occasion, to make things happen, to move forward with excellence, and to make a difference. He wanted his people to go out and "delight the customers" with the solutions they needed from the company.

Every team member was moved by the CEO's caring and powerful words. They committed to make the necessary changes and work together with clear lines of communication and collaboration in order to drive toward the successful outcome. His ability to paint a clear picture of his expectations was a powerful motivator for everyone in the room. In the months that followed, people worked together, clear lines of communication were established, and mutual buy-in of strategy was achieved – a great foundation for an excellent outcome for all.

The answers to these three questions will help you to be a highly effective and influential communicator.

1) How can I be more appropriately transparent and honest when communicating with others?

_____

_____

_____

2) What will help me communicate with clarity and exchange clear information with others?

_____

_____

_____

3) When engaged in dialogue with others, how can I listen to them with my best intent and understand what they are communicating to me?

_____

_____

_____

To become a better listener:

- Pay attention to what the other person is saying and choose to assume they have good intent (you will be able to identify ill intent quickly – it will show up).
- Ask clarifying questions before responding unfavorably or negatively.
- Be responsible for your own emotions and reactions.

COMPETENCE
Communicate with your highest level of clarity

Today – Focus on the way you convey your thoughts, views, judgments, and opinions with others:
<u>Look for ways to be –</u>

- Honest when communicating
- Precise and reasonable when exchanging information
- Understanding of others when listening

<u>Read the above at least three times today.</u>
What do the statements mean to you?

How will you incorporate their meaning into your daily interactions with others?

WEEK 2 / WEDNESDAY

CONSISTENCY
Create an effective strategy

A consistent person is known for being reliable. They are able to build trust with others by creating predictable structures, systems, and measurable results. They also have the ability to stabilize situations.

> **"People need to find their own language for describing
> the intent of their efforts in ways that work in their own context,
> as part of developing their own strategies and leadership practices."**
> PETER SENGE
> SENIOR LECTURER AT THE MIT SLOAN SCHOOL OF MANAGEMENT

Creating an effective strategy for success involves two levels of learning, according to Peter Senge. In addition to lecturing at the MIT Sloan School of Management, Senge founded the Society for Organizational Learning and has written many books about leadership and management.

His teachings support two ways of reasoning about learning:

- The first level of learning builds your skill sets and produces results from effectively using those skills.
- The second, deeper level helps you develop your capabilities so they are reliable, predictable, and reproducible.

Your leadership skills can create the opportunity to provide direction and management of others by providing systems that are reliable, consistent, and predictable. Practicing good strategies will produce desired outcomes. There are no quick fixes when discovering the proper strategies or action plans for a particular situation and problem. The following thoughts will help you to build a consistent and trustworthy strategy both personally and professionally:

- Be honest with yourself
  What established methods are really working for you?

- Use an approach with purpose
  What form of communication or message are you really sending to others?

- Assess the accuracy of your information
  Are you using updated material, facts and data?

- Evaluate your own predictability
  Are you really creating consistent behaviors that build trust with others?

Effective strategy does not have to be groundbreaking. It just has to work and bring results for the situation, people, or issues that need to be solved.

Effective strategy is not just something to think about. It is something you plan and choose to consistently refine for greater results.

Tess' Client Creates A New Strategy

One of my clients was hired for a new job at a very large organization. He had researched companies with whose vision and mission statements he agreed. As he narrowed his interest to three companies, he began to research people he knew in these organizations through social media.

Part of his strategy was to make connections with people who had worked at these companies or were still employed by them. As he scheduled meetings to ask questions about the companies' leadership, employees, and culture, he gathered a wealth of information to help him narrow his focus and choose with which company he would prefer to work.

The information he gathered from his connections proved to be helpful when preparing for his interviews. Ultimately, he was offered a great job at the company of his choice.

Why was it such a great opportunity? He was offered a job that fit his expertise and competence.

After a few months on the job, he found these things out about the company:

- Its leadership is trustworthy, and it accurately represented itself throughout the hiring process and orientation.
- The Company is committed to further training, equipping its employees to increase their competencies so they are capable of doing their work effectively.
- The cross-functional teams are willing to collaborate and its members are willing to help and mentor one another. My client found his niche in his new job, which provided the opportunity to contribute at his highest level for the best results. As his contributions influenced outcomes in his department, others within the organization began to take notice of his good work. His consistent work builds trust with others within the organization. Also, it brought an award, recognizing his knowledge, expertise and willingness to help his department add value to the entire organization.

During a coaching session, I asked him, "What strategy is working for you in your new job?" He communicated this:

- "Every Friday, I prioritize what I need to get done at the beginning of the following week.
- "Every Sunday evening, I go to bed early. I need to feel rested and ready for Monday.
- "Monday, I go in an hour early to get a head start on my day and focus on priority number one.
- "If I can leave work at a reasonable time on Monday evening, I go for a run – exercise is important for me to stay mentally and physically healthy.
- "Tuesday, I complete priority number one, if I did not get it done on Monday, and begin working on priority number two.

- "Wednesday, I follow up on priority number one, complete or follow up on priority number two, and begin working on priority number three.
- "By Thursday, I am following up on all of my priorities and others that have come up during the week.
- "On Friday, I make sure the work that I can complete is done and strategize for the beginning of the next week. Typically, I use Friday to further connect with employees, peers and co-workers, in order to stay connected and involved with them."

Certainly, my client's schedule is significantly more complex than he described. Yet, he has simplified his strategy to provide focus on his true priorities. He is intentional in what he needs to get done every day, and he utilizes tools to help him stay focused and productive in the context of his role and responsibilities.

How would you describe your current strategy for your primary responsibilities at work?

_____

_____

_____

_____

How would you describe your current strategy for dealing with your primary responsibilities in your home life?

_____

_____

_____

_____

How would you describe your ability to stay focused on one thing to completion?

_____

_____

CONSISTENCY
Create An Effective Strategy

Today, focus on your approach when accomplishing tasks:
<u>Make sure your –</u>

- **Procedures are producing results**
  Be honest with yourself and others.

- **Approach has purpose**
  First impressions are important.

- **Routines create predictability**
  This builds trust with others.

- **Current information is updated and accurate**
  You will need to assess and research.

<u>Read the above at least three times today.</u>
What do the statements mean to you?

_____

_____

How will you incorporate their meaning into your daily interactions with others?

_____

WEEK 2 / THURSDAY

CREATIVITY
Stay Curious

An influential person has the ability to create strong relationships and build trust with others. They are able to think of new ideas and process input with others. Their solutions produce excellent outcomes for the good of themselves and others.

> **"Relationships are at the heart and center
> of the capitalist system, both contractual relationships and
> deeper, more enabling covenantal relationships."**
> MAX DEPREE, FORMER PRESIDENT AND CEO
> OF HERMAN MILLER AND AUTHOR OF "LEADERSHIP IS AN ART"

Staying curious is a cultivated habit that creates compelling experiences with others. When we are interested in others, we are curious about who they are and what they do. Curiosity is part of the foundation that builds every one of our relationships.

Tess' Curiosity Leads to a Rich Life

I often commute back and forth from L.A. to New York City. I typically don't remember the pilots, flight attendants, or people on the planes. Because I fly certain airlines consistently, there are times I have remembered the flight attendants. Normally, I use the flight time for work or to personally re-energize by resting or reading. There have been exceptions when a dialogue will begin with the person sitting next to me. Mutual curiosity between us sometimes keeps the conversation going throughout the flight.

On one of these flights, I met an incredibly talented and creative woman who is a producer. She boarded the plane visibly stressed. My thought process presented a couple of options: "Ignore this stressed-out person next to me or try to engage her and see where the conversation goes."

I chose to engage her and asked, "Are you okay; is there anything I can do to help?" I further explained my profession as an executive leadership coach. We began to talk about what was going on in her life, her burnout from work and need to change things up. Hearing about her world of producing, directing, and marketing was fascinating. The conversation continued throughout the flight to the point it started to become more personal. We even found out we shared a similar start in life – we are both adopted. How we got to this level of communicating with one another, I really can't remember – I just remember staying curious about who she was as a person and how she was living her life.

Today, I continue to be privileged to call her a dear friend. We have stayed curious about one another's lives, and that continued curiosity has led us to enriching each other's lives. We bring our unique differences, our ways of thinking, ways of making decisions and ways of living out our lives with meaning. These differences make us more interested in and supportive of one another.

Typically, you build relationships because you share an interest in learning more about the other. Once you become curious about someone and want more information, the relationship begins to grow in both depth and breadth, often in ways you did not expect. As you experience life within the context of those relationships that have evolved from curiosity, you grow and develop together within them. As long as you stay curious, every one of your relationships has the potential to impact you in profound ways.

How curious are you about your relationships? Take a personal inventory:

- Are your personal and professional relationships satisfying?
  Do they feel comfortable, encouraging, and beneficial to you?
  Why or why not?

  _____

  _____

- Are your professional and personal relationships a series of starts and stops?
  Do they feel unpredictable?
  Why or why not?

  _____

  _____

- Are your personal and professional relationships bogged down?
  Do they feel burdensome?
  Why or why not?

  _____

  _____

- Do your professional and personal relationships feel empty?
  Do you feel disengaged?
  Why or why not?

  _____

  _____

Healthy relationships need your personal investment of curiosity. This includes asking thoughtful questions to learn and know more about each other. Curiosity includes gathering information for connection and gratification. It is a willingness to learn and be life-giving. It is being the kind of person who finds other people more interesting, rather than wanting people to find you the most interesting person in the room.

You can learn to be curious about others. As a leader of your own self with a blueprint that includes being curious about others and their personal and professional experiences, you will find yourself more interesting to people as well.

We have found this to be consistently true when asking questions:

- People enjoy talking about their lives and work. They like to share their life experiences, what they are doing, how they do things, and what works for them.
- The answers and comments you gather give you clues as to what is important to the other person.
- As you ask questions, listen to their answers. You will recognize common themes, patterns, and habits, which will help you to communicate at a higher level.

We suggest you use a very simple tool when building intentional relationships, be they with family, friend, or business associate:

1) Begin with "why?"
   Why is this relationship important to you?

Write your thoughts below:

_____
_____
_____

2) Move to "how?"
   How are you going to invest in this important relationship?

Write your thoughts below:

_____
_____
_____

3) Close with "what?"
   What are the outcomes you desire for this important relationship?

Write your thoughts below:

_____
_____
_____

An Unplanned Friendship

My husband, Dean, is a Realtor. Several years ago, he sold a piece of property for his clients in the beautiful Santa Ynez valley outside of Santa Barbara, California. The property is atop a hill overlooking twenty-three acres of wild oak trees, rolling hills and wild flowers. I call the home and property "a little piece of heaven on Earth." It is gorgeous! There are nearby wineries, horse properties, and farms. It is a place to unwind and unplug amid the beauty of nature.

When the property sold to a foreign buyer, Dean became acquainted with the new homeowner since he knew everything about the home. The new owner relied on him as he began to make renovations and make the home his own.

In the process, Dean and I became friends with the new owner. We found our new friend interesting, intellectual, and well traveled, with a good sense of humor and an appreciation for good food and wine.

The friendship continues, with fond memories of patio dining by the pool at all times of year. The new owner enjoys Dean's cooking, and we are all pleased with the abundance of excellent locally grown food and wines. Since the new owner spends eight months living abroad, he relies on Dean to check on the property. Believe me, it is not a hardship to spend the weekend at the house in Santa Ynez and make sure everything is okay.

We all have stayed curious about the lives we each live and the contributions we make to the friendship. It was an unplanned friendship, yet, as we gathered new knowledge about one another and learned from one another, our shared experience became part of our "memory," allowing us to build history and trust with one another.

In her book, "Rising Strong," Brene Brown says this about leadership and relationships:

"The most transformative and resilient leaders that I've worked with over the course of my career have three things in common: First, they recognize the central role that relationships and story play in culture and strategy, and they stay curious about their own emotions, thoughts, and behaviors. Second, they understand and stay curious about how emotions, thoughts, and behaviors are connected in the people they lead, and how those factors affect relationships and perception. And, third, they have the ability and willingness to lean in to discomfort and vulnerability."

You are the leader of yourself when it comes to staying curious about others and building the relationships that are meaningful to you. Keep asking good questions, as it is quite possible a good answer will bring a relationship into an interesting and expanding existence.

CREATIVITY
Stay Curious

Today - Focus on being eager to know something new:

- Show interest in others – ask thoughtful questions
- Gather new information from others
- Be a learner wanting more, not less, information

<u>Read the above at least three times today.</u>
What do the statements mean to you?

_____

_____

How will you incorporate their meaning into your daily interactions with others?

_____

WEEK 2 / FRIDAY

CONFIDENCE
Unlocking Your Potential

A person who possesses confidence personally and professionally builds trust with others. The quality of their communication is high, and they excel when resolving conflicts. They are able to influence others through listening, gathering feedback, and collaborating with others to find solutions for best results. Confidence is fully realized through the development of the first four C's.

A Review of Your Learning:

Reflect on how you have been able to unlock your potential in the areas mentioned above? Write your thoughts below:

- **Raising the bar - Character**

  _____
  _____
  _____
  _____

- **Communicating with clarity - Competence**

  _____
  _____
  _____
  _____

- **Developing effective strategies - Consistency**

  _____
  _____
  _____
  _____

- **Being curious - Creativity**

  _____
  _____
  _____
  _____

After thinking about these areas in which you've discovered new potential, how confident do you feel?

_____

_____

_____

_____

"Put your future in good hands – your own."
MARK VICTOR HANSEN
MOTIVATIONAL SPEAKER

CONFIDENCE
Unlocking Your Potential

Today – Focus on the past four days as you have built your CONFIDENCE through unlocking your potential:

<u>Being incredible (choose to be amazing) and raising the bar for yourself and others by –</u>

- Communicating with your highest level of clarity
- Developing and using effective strategies
- Staying curious in relationships

<u>Read the above at least three times today.</u>
What do the statements mean to you?

_____

_____

How will you incorporate their meaning into your daily interactions with others?

_____

WEEK 3 / MONDAY

CHARACTER
Admit Responsibility for Failures and Mistakes

A person of character knows who they are and why they do what they do. They are able to build trust with others through their integrity, trustworthiness, and honesty.

"Before leaders can do the right things,
they have to know how to do them."
JAMES M. KOUZES AND BARRY Z. POSNER
"CREDIBILITY: HOW LEADERS GAIN AND LOSE IT; WHY PEOPLE DEMAND IT"

Stephen Covey writes, "We have the initiative and the responsibility to make things happen … we have the ability to choose our response to our responsibilities." Accepting responsibility for your life is the highest form of human maturity. It is about having a good character.

Dan Grows Up With a Gratitude Deficit

I grew up in a home where the general tone of the conversation was one of negativity and complaints. By the time I left home, you might guess that my own head was filled with negativity and that I easily blamed others for my misfortunes, but this was not the case. Thankfully, I escaped this paradigm.

I don't remember exactly when, but very early on I discovered personal development speaker Jim Rohn. His books and lectures helped me realize no one but me was responsible for my destiny. Over the years, I've learned how counterproductive complaining is. It's literally time thrown in the trash that could have been spent on achieving a more productive outcome.

I've even gone to the extreme of taking personal responsibility for EVERYTHING in my life. No matter what happens, I am constantly reflecting on things I could have done or said to achieve a different outcome. To give up responsibility is to hand away control of my own destiny.

Think about and ask yourself, "What would you like to change?" Write it down:

_____

_____

_____

_____

_____

If you choose a paradigm of complaining, a mindset of blaming others, and a habit of failing to take responsibility, you choose to place all control outside of your own influence. If you do this, we guarantee that nothing in your life will change.

You are responsible for leading yourself. As Stephen Covey says, "Proactive people recognize that they are 'response-able.'" Be a leader who is response-able and one who accepts responsibility. When choosing to accept responsibility, the mindset of marginal gains or incremental change is helpful – remember how it works: Take baby steps toward changing behaviors that no longer work for you or increasing behaviors that will help you to be more successful.

Whether you need to stop complaining and blaming, you need to add the behavior of helping others with a good attitude, or some other habit that needs correction and take this first step: Change your paradigm and attitude. Then choose a specific action step: Be intentional with your first positive action and you will have begun to shift your abilities toward effective change. If you pay attention this will also give you opportunities to discover and implement new ideas.

Tess Uncovers Some Incongruence

During one of my training sessions, a leader in attendance exclaimed, "I'm not going to admit responsibility for failures and mistakes to others because my responsibility is to find solutions to failures and mistakes!" Granted, he had a fair argument, but his 360 Feedback from his CEO, Sr. Executive Team and co-workers, indicated his need to build trust and transparency with them. His ability to admit his mistakes and failures was key to gaining the trust of all.

Life and work come with problems to be solved. You may find yourself asking, "Am I responsible for solving all of my life and work problems alone?" Not necessarily. When living and working with others, it is important to assess who is responsible and accountable for solving specific issues or problems. Determine which problems require input and ideas from others so you can solve the problem(s) together.

There are times the problems are managed by independent analysis and can be solved by your decision-making abilities. There are other times the problems are managed by finding a solution with a compromise made with others. You concede something that is important to you and the other person concedes something that is important to them. Overall, the concession moves you both forward towards the desired outcomes and both parties are satisfied. And, there are times the solutions to problems are quite complex. It requires the input, thoughts and feedback of others with knowledge and expertise that you, as one individual does not have and yet, collectively you and the group are able to make a sound and good decision.

While the leader mentioned above was fine with solving problems on his own, he was less willing to work with others and be accountable to them for his own actions and culpability. Do you see the difference?

You can be both responsible and response-able for solving problems on your own, with no accountability to others. This may or may not result in acceptable solutions for all.

Or, you can be responsible and response-able for solving problems with others while being accountable to one another. When people are mutually accountable, they have a greater capacity for lasting change. Why is this true? The mutually accountability requires a greater depth of dialogue. When you are solving problems on your own, there is no dialogue with others and decisions are made with your own personal interpretation of the problem, which may or may not be accurate. You are not able to fully grasp the accuracy of your own paradigm and solution to the problem, until you hear the thoughts and views of others.

A mature leader who exhibits strong character is willing to admit to, and share responsibility for, failures and mistakes, and to be a part of the solution. This kind of leader has the ability to build trust with others. Trust increases collaborative efforts and the possibility of good solutions for all.

As you lead your life personally and professionally, admitting your own errors will build your credibility and give you the opportunity to create strategies for immediate, corrective action.

A first step in righting wrongs is to admit the truth to yourself. When you know that you were wrong, do the right thing and admit your mistake(s). Blaming others is misleading your own thought process and self-justifying your actions. Blame is completely unproductive and wastes valuable time for everyone.

You know people who cannot and will not admit that they are wrong (and who, frankly, are difficult to be around for very long). Stay focused on your own behavior and do the right thing. Transparency creates a healthy dialogue, "Yes, I made a mistake". Your appropriate vulnerability – a willingness to admit when you are wrong is a key attribute to your character. Your honesty will build your capacity to be a responsible and trustworthy leader.

Who would you rather work with and for? Someone who admits to and learns from mistakes or someone who always passes the buck to others?

Here are important questions leaders should ask when seeking solutions:

- Do I really listen to the input and opinions of others?
- Where should I have gathered more knowledge or understanding of the issue(s)?
- How should I have been more collaborative with my team?
- Whose talent and skill did I miss or overlook?
- Could I have done anything differently under the circumstances?

Build your personal and professional self-awareness and knowledge.
In what scenario are you most dependable?

_____
_____

How well do you take personal responsibility?

_____
_____

How often do you find yourself blaming someone other than yourself?

_____
_____

Are you able to build trust with others through being appropriately vulnerable and transparent?

_____
_____

Where are you willing to grow and develop in building trust with others?

_____

_____

Choose to model the behavior you want for yourself and others. When others hear you admit failures or mistakes, they will have more confidence to admit their own. What a great concept: Truth will lead you to greater success! The more responsibility you take for modeling best behaviors, mastering your skills, and being confident in your own learning, the stronger your foundation for success will be.

CHARACTER
Admit Responsibility for Failures and Mistakes

Today – Focus on acknowledging truth by being a person who is...

- **Accountable to others**
- **Dependable**
- **Willing to grow and develop**
- **Able and willing to make wise decisions**

<u>Read the above at least three times today.</u>
What do the statements mean to you?

_____

_____

How will you incorporate their meaning into your daily interactions with others?

_____

<u>WEEK 3 / TUESDAY</u>

COMPETENCE
Prioritize and Manage Your Time

A person of competence understands the reality of their skills and knows how they bring value to their relationships and work with their expertise. They are able to build trust with others through their well-known capabilities, qualifications, and experiences.

> **"Things which matter most
> must never be at the mercy
> of things which matter least."**
> JOHANN WOLFGANG VON GOETHE

It is possible that you have heard a saying along the lines of "Just because you're busy doesn't mean you're being productive." Our busy schedules can create stress and tension, which rarely help us function at our best.

The gift of a new day is the opportunity to decide, "Am I going to be just a busybody or am I going to be productive with a focus on what is most important?" We want you to look beyond being "busy" and work to develop a personal philosophy of productivity.

Assess your capabilities with the following questions. Answer yes or no.

1) Am I capable of seeing and responding to new opportunities? _____
2) Am I capable of making room and clearing the clutter or busyness in order to respond to new opportunities? _____
3) Am I capable of delegating to others and eliminating activities that no longer add high value to my philosophy, vision, and mission? _____

If you answered yes to all of the questions, stay the course. You are on the right track with a healthy mindset and behaviors so keep reading.

If you answered no to one or more, you may be sending mixed signals to others. Continue reading, as you will want to create a healthy mindset and behaviors.

At this point in your reading, you have been gaining knowledge and understanding, and you are coming to see that clarity and predictability set you up for success. However, your "busy" actions may speak louder than your words. If you're ineffectively busy too much of the time, your philosophy, vision, and mission will probably be lost amid your frenetic activity.

Dan's Leveraging Competence to Create a Dominant Sales Force

One of the central tenets of my sales training is to create a specific plan for salespeople that maximizes the amount of time they get to spend face-to-face with buyers. My salespeople end up sitting in front of more buyers than those of our competitors, which means my team wins more often.

Lots of salespeople in my industry do not have a plan of any kind. They may have a general idea of where they are going each day, but nothing is set. They have an attitude of going with the flow and responding in the moment, with no plan. This casual behavior and spontaneously reacting in a moments notice sounds good on the surface, until you look at the benefits of having a plan and agenda.

The difference between having a plan or not is this: In the time my salespeople will meet with 100 buyers who are expecting them, our competitor salespeople will try frantically to meet with 50 buyers who aren't expecting them in the same amount of time. The difference in output and productivity is enormous. Our intentional plan creates predictability, which is a quality of our competence. It is our competence that provides our buyers the highest level of service.

Having a competent plan can mean the difference between incredible accomplishments and abject failures.

Tess' Commitment to Extreme Competence

Years ago, I was in graduate school in Pasadena, California, and my daughter was attending college in Seattle. At one point, we realized that we were both on track to graduate on the same date in the same year. As I talked about this dilemma with my husband and daughter, we devised two plans:

- Support our daughter in her graduation and forgo participating in mine.
- Drastically rearrange my schedule, take 50 units the following year, and graduate a year early.

The two plans would require very different courses of action.

I chose strategy number two. Was I insane? Probably! But, I was driven both by the desire to celebrate success and a personal philosophy of productivity. Here are the methods that supported my strategic decision:

- I cut my work schedule to part-time and attended class full-time. Yes, not everyone has this option, and yes, my husband and I agreed to make financial sacrifices to make this happen.
- I was focused every minute of every day for 14 months, and my schedule was grueling.
- I delegated my responsibilities to those who were able and capable. I had to make certain sacrifices in my career, socially, and at home.
- I had a system for every day (and it often felt like for every minute), and what I needed to accomplish to reach my goal. I recognized that following the system was absolutely necessary even though I don't consider myself a "systems" person.

As challenging as this period was, it was actually invigorating to be so focused on one thing – learning and finishing my courses so I could graduate. I knew my goal would allow me to more quickly respond to new career opportunities in the future.

So how did it all work out? We were able to attend both graduations! The opportunity to celebrate each of our special days was a beautiful experience and a meaningful memory for all of us. To this day, I am thankful that I stayed focused on my philosophy, goal, and plan, which allowed me to accomplish all of my priorities.

The following exercise helped me to focus and stay the course in order to reach my goal. Use this as a template to complete the exercise that follows.

My values and activities during my time of focused attention on graduate work were the following (and they still hold true today):

1) Commitment to my spouse – I value honest, open, and supportive communication in our "true companion" relationship.

2) Commitment to my children – I value honest, open, and supportive communication as I continue to build my relationships with them. As their mom, I am available to them 24-7 (no matter what their age).

3) Commitment to my personal faith – I value my faith and I believe in the strength I draw from it.

4) Commitment to my education – I value learning on all levels and how it gives breadth and depth to my life. Learning is never wasted on me, as I'm willing to discover new ways of thinking, develop new strategies, and deliver great outcomes.

5) Commitment to my work – I value the opportunity to contribute at the highest level and am willing to be stretched to go above and beyond what I can possibly imagine.

6) Commitment to my extended family and friends – they were very understanding and supportive, more so than I could give them in return at the time.

Setting Priorities and Focus

List your top five values (family, health, and spiritual):

1) _____
2) _____
3) _____
4) _____
5) _____

List the top five activities that affect what you value (hobbies, interests, and clubs):

1) _____
2) _____
3) _____
4) _____
5) _____

Of these 10 values and activities, rank your top 5 in order of importance:

1) _____
2) _____
3) _____
4) _____
5) _____

Of your top five values and activities, why are these important to you?

_____
_____
_____
_____
_____
_____

Do you need to create a plan for your top five values and activities to experience them more fully?

If so, choose one of your top five values and activities. Create a six-point plan of action (like the one written above) and give yourself permission to focus on your value or activity for a period of time. See what you discover about yourself and about what is important to you.

1) _____
_____

2) _____
_____

3) _____
_____

4) _____
_____

5) _____
_____

6) _____
_____

It may be helpful for you to take some time and reflect on what you need to change –you may want to rethink what will help you to focus and plan more effectively.

_____

_____

_____

_____

_____

_____

COMPETENCE
Prioritize and Manage Your Time

Today – Focus on the people and things that are the most important in your life:

<u>Create –</u>

- A list of priorities
- A ranking of those priorities
- A schedule with a focus on achieving those priorities
- A plan to handle difficult situations that should not be avoided or ignored

<u>Read the above at least three times today.</u>
What do the statements mean to you?

_____

_____

How will you incorporate their meaning into your daily interactions with others?

_____

WEEK 3 / WEDNESDAY

CONSISTENCY
Keep Commitments

A consistent person is known for being reliable. They are able to build trust with others by creating predictable structures, systems, and measurable results. They also have the ability to stabilize situations.

> **"Your ultimate success in business and in life**
> **depends on how well you know yourself,**
> **what you value, and why you value it."**
> JAMES M. KOUZES AND BARRY Z. POSNER
> (FROM "LEADERSHIP BEGINS WITH AN INNER JOURNEY,"
> ESSAY IN THE JOURNAL LEADER TO LEADER)

Nothing will kill your credibility faster than if you are perceived as a flake – as being predictably unpredictable and as someone who never follows through.

When you start to slip from full commitment, it is almost impossible to climb back to credibility. People will focus more on whether they can count on you than on your expertise, skill sets, and work.

In the book "Influencer," the authors tell a wonderful story about commitment by Dr. Mimi Silbert, the founder of Delancey Street Foundation. The foundation is filled with mostly "gang members, thieves, prostitutes, robbers, and murderers," says Silbert. "Typical new hires have had 18 felony convictions. They've been homeless for years, and most are lifetime drug addicts. Within hours of joining Delancey, they are working in a restaurant, moving company, car repair shop, or one of the many Delancey companies … Of those who join Delancey, over 90 percent never go back to drugs or crime. Instead they earn degrees, become professionals, and change their lives. Forever." She facilitates this remarkable change through the power of influence. Every person who enters Delancey Street is empowered to train and mentor others. Each individual is responsible for equipping someone new with the skills to do their particular job, along with being held accountable for the outcomes of their job.

The "big picture" of Silbert's leadership is her ability to create a system that empowers, trains, mentor's, hold accountable, and influences the behaviors of the "gang members, thieves, prostitutes, robbers and murderers". The consistency is what drives her and her organization to follow through and earn great outcomes.

Your "big picture" leadership story will very likely, look different from Silbert's. Yet, each of us has a story of either consistency or inconsistency in our personal leadership experience.

Where have you had an opportunity to demonstrate your commitment to a group of people, job, or organization?

_____

_____

Where have you found yourself to be inconsistent in commitment and actions?

_____

_____

Write a brief account of your consistent leadership story or your struggle with consistency below:

_____
_____
_____
_____
_____
_____
_____
_____
_____
_____
_____
_____

Dr. Mimi Silbert's leadership quality begins with her commitment to her personal values and beliefs – her character. As leader of yourself, you are driven by your core personal values and beliefs, as well. That focus is the way you stay committed and responsible.

As you are committed and responsible for your leadership, you build personal self-awareness and self-management of your behaviors.

When you are faced with challenges, your personal self-awareness gives you the ability to understand the truth of the situation. The truth will give you clarity about your reality. And, clarity with the understanding of reality will give you confidence to make the best decisions in the context of the situation. You will be mindfully aware of the potential impacts on you and others from the decisions you make.

When you are committed to your values and who you are as a leader, you take charge of your life and you act responsibly. Without your commitment to your values and who you are, you will lack clarity of understanding of "why" you do what you do. When you lack clarity, you lack a sense of true reality, which has the ability to render you ineffective and your behaviors will follow your lack of clarity.

Be the leader others seek and look forward to working with by implementing this strategy for staying committed and consistent:

- Keep your promises
  If you can't keep a promise, don't make it.

- Follow through on your obligations
  If you can't follow through on obligations, don't put yourself in the position of being obligated.

- Display loyalty
  If you can't be loyal, take a hard look at your true values.

- Maintain a high standard of dedication
  If you can't be dedicated, ask yourself why not. What is stopping you?

A Helpful Tool:

DWYSYWD: Do What You Say You Will Do

When you are trustworthy, others will believe in your intent and your ability to follow through on your commitments. Ultimately, your leadership is unquestionable because you do what you say you will do. As you are consistent and connected to others, your leadership motivates and empowers others to do what you want them to do.

BEGINNING TO CREATE YOUR LEADERSHIP BLUEPRINT:

Creating your leadership blueprint is a process and it begins with you writing down your thoughts about the following questions. There are no right or wrong answers as you continue to discover the following: who you are, what your values and beliefs are, what your influences are and what makes you happy.

We encourage you to write what first comes to mind. There is no need to edit yourself or try to create perfect sentences. Give yourself permission to think out loud and write your thoughts…

Know who you are. What are your character strengths?

_____
_____
_____
_____

What values and beliefs do you really care about?

_____
_____
_____
_____

Who has influenced you and shaped your attitudes?

_____
_____
_____
_____

What life philosophy makes you happy?

_____
_____
_____
_____

You are in charge of your personal and professional story – your leadership story. Leading your own life gives you strength and it requires you to face your own challenges.

The following questions help you define what is positive and best for you.

When you are at your best, committed to your life, relationships and work…how do you want your life, relationships and work to look?

_____

_____

_____

_____

_____

_____

What do you want the next chapters of your story to look like?

_____

_____

_____

_____

What title would you give your personal and professional story?

_____

CONSISTENCY
Keep Commitments

Today – Focus on being fully responsible for your outcomes:
<u>**You will be more effective when you –**</u>

- **Keep your promises**
- **Follow through on your obligations**
- **Display loyalty**
- **Maintain a high standard of dedication**

<u>**Read the above at least three times today.**</u>
What do the statements mean to you?

_____

_____

How will you incorporate their meaning into your daily interactions with others?

_____

WEEK 3 / THURSDAY

CREATIVITY
Overcome Obstacles

An influential person has the ability to create strong relationships and build trust with others. They are able to think of new ideas and process input with others. Their solutions produce excellent outcomes for the good of themselves and others.

"Yeah, but my situation's more difficult than that!"
KERRY PATTERSON, JOSEPH GRENNY, RON MCMILLAN, AL SWITZLER
AUTHORS OF "CRUCIAL CONVERSATIONS"

**"Life is a series of sales situations,
and the answer is 'no' if you don't ask."**
PATRICIA FRIPP, EXECUTIVE SPEECH COACH

Dan Learns to Love Rejection

As a business-to-business salesperson for more than a decade, I can tell you, I've been rejected over ten thousand times! Seriously. When rejection happens, I have two options:

- Accept rejection and hang my head
  or
- Learn from rejection and use the opportunity to creatively adjust my approach and forge a new path

I am happy to say that I have chosen option two the vast majority of the time. I am certain that this is the primary reason I have increased my ability to be creative in overcoming obstacles

Most salespeople would agree with the statement, "Sales is a numbers game." So how does a "numbers game" involve creativity, rejection and overcoming obstacles? Everything! Creativity is the motivator to create a plan and goals.

This means that the more strategic you are in the number of people you talk to, the more sales you ultimately develop. You have to create the opportunity to talk to hundreds, if not thousands, of people to be moderately successful and tens of thousands to be wildly successful. Despite this generally accepted fact, that sales is developing opportunities to connect with people and build relationships, many salespeople work as if they had never heard the statement, "Sales is a number game." Nor do they see the need to be creative in their approach when accepting rejection and overcoming the negative interactions with potential customers.

Think about this, the numbers game is not just for salespeople. It is for you, as well.

If you create and …

- Have a long-term plan
- Break down that plan into daily activity goals
- Work each day to reach those activity goals

What will happen?

You will soon be thriving in the areas that are most important to you.

For a salesperson who realizes the challenges of the numbers game and wants to win by increasing their chances of success, three things become evident:

- Obstacles are opportunities to creatively solve problems.
- Creativity is essential for the best outcome.
- Sales is all about building a relationship with your customer! And, you may need to be creative to build a strong relationship.

At some point, every plan or goal will face obstacles. The ways in which you choose to face them will strengthen or weaken the qualities of your leadership. Solving problems gives you the choice to create healthy and meaningful dialogue with others and the opportunity to solve problems together. This can also increase your creativity, as there are many different approaches to successfully solving conflict or problems.

> **"The same wind blows on us all.**
> **The economic wind,**
> **the social wind,**
> **the political wind.**
> **The same wind blows on everybody …**
> **The difference in where you arrive**
> **in one year, three years, five years,**
> **the difference in arrival**
> **is not the blowing of the wind,**
> **but the set of the sail."**
> JIM ROHN, ENTREPRENEUR

COACHING QUESTIONS:

We know that overcoming obstacles is challenging and you may feel the least creative when feeling stressed to solve problems. The following questions are designed to give you an opportunity to reflect on what holds you back from solving problems creatively and effectively. This exercise will help you reflect on what will work for you.

What are two things that are working well for you when faced with overcoming obstacles?

1) _____

_____

2) _____

_____

Great! Keep doing these two things.
What are one or two excuses that you tend to frequently use to explain why things are not happening for you?

1) _____

_____

2) _____

_____

What are one or two obstacles standing in your way and creating the greatest confusion as you try to move forward?

1) _____

_____

2) _____

_____

What would help you to creatively find solutions to those obstacles?

1) _____

_____

2) _____

_____

What is the first step toward using your creative solutions?

1) _____
   _____

Options With Different Outcomes:

The following statements indicate the probability of how you choose to solve problems. The way you process problems is unique to you and will have different outcomes depending on your preferences.

Which statement more closely exemplifies your style?

- I prefer to address difficulties that are bothering me with others.
  or
- I prefer to avoid issues and problems.

When solving problems,

- I prefer to embrace good solutions with others and move forward together.
  or
- I prefer to find my own solutions and move forward independently.

The statements you choose will indicate your ability to build a creative dialogue with others or a lack of desire to build a creative dialogue. Also, your choices will reflect how you like to move forward with good solutions with others or independently and on your own. Each approach will lead you in the direction of a unique outcome.

The answers to these statements are meant to build your self-awareness, "why you do what you do." As you reflect on your "why", you have the opportunity to ask yourself this question, "What creative outcomes do I really want to experience?" And, "With whom do I need to help me find creative solutions?"

Creating A Blueprint for Dialogue

Would you agree that some problems actually can, be solved on your own, while others require a dialogue with others? As Dan mentioned in the opening of this daily read, rejection is part of a salesperson's life. The most skilled professional salesperson can have a really bad day and lose a customer to a competitor. Ouch! It's possible the ability to create a dialogue at a crucial time was lost by the salesperson.

The fear of rejection is real in any relationship. And, it is quite probable the fear of rejection or handling things poorly holds you back from creating a positive dialogue and healthy solutions to problems with others.

Below we have outlined a way for you to expand your ability and create a safe dialogue with another person. The likelihood of a good, healthy outcome is increased with your ability to create and use your mind, your heart and your words without the fear of rejection and obstacles getting in the way.

The concepts come from two resources: "Crucial Conversations" by Kerry Patterson, Joseph Grenny, Ron McMillan, and Al Switzler and "Just Listen" by Mark Goulston.

1. Choose an agreed-upon place in which to meet.

2. Take turns communicating your thoughts, views, and opinions.
    - Ask questions, remembering that you want to understand what the other person is communicating before sharing your own thoughts.
    - Listen with integrity and humility.
    - Show interest in the views of the other person.
    - Mirror and dissolve the barriers between you and the other person with healthy emotionally controlled reactions. Mirroring is simply putting yourself in harmony with another person in posture, speech patterns, volume of voice, etc.
    - Reflect back what you heard the person communicate.

The authors of "Crucial Conversations" call this the "pool of shared meaning." Can you visualize a beautiful pool with crystal-blue water? It's peaceful, right? Now, visualize a rapidly running stream and flowing water. As cool as this may appear, there is a lot of chaos going on beneath the water. Our conversations can be peaceful or chaotic, depending on how we stay focused and control our emotions.

3. Watch when conditions change and resistance creeps in.
    - Be honest and say, "I think we are moving away from our original topic."
    - Ask, "Would you agree we are finding it challenging to stay on topic?"
    - State, "Why don't we give ourselves a break and come back together in 30 minutes to talk about our disagreement?"

4. When returning to the dialogue, continue to take turns sharing thoughts, views, and opinions.
    - Reflect, with respect, what you hear the person saying to you.
    - Continue to show a genuine interest in the other person.
    - Move the dialogue toward a solution and ask, "Would you consider _____ as an option in solving our problem?"

5. Your dialogue should end with both parties:
    - Feeling understood by the other
    - Buying in to the solution
    - Willing to move toward an agreed-upon action
    - Agreeing to a time frame for solving the issue

As you lead yourself well to overcome obstacles with another person or group, do yourself a favor and know the patterns that occur when you lose control. No solutions occur when you are emotionally out of control. You may create a situation where someone will flee from you, disengage with you, and does not want to re-engage at all. Your best option is to manage and lead your emotions through a difficult dialogue and find the best solutions for the problems with others.

Managing your emotions is difficult. It is difficult because you are contending with your immediate instincts to fight or flee. Hitting the emotional "pause button" requires a trained, mindful and controlled response.

When the "stakes are high, emotions are strong, and opinions vary ..."
KERRY PATTERSON, JOSEPH GRENNY, RON MCMILLAN, AL SWITZLER
AUTHORS OF "CRUCIAL CONVERSATIONS"

"Get yourself under control first"
"JUST LISTEN"
MARK GOULSTON

Tess' Client Finds Emotional Balance

I coached a client who scored extremely high on the "Feeling" side of the Myers/Briggs personality profile (the Myers/Briggs is an assessment to describe 16 personality types with the focus on building individual self-awareness and self-managed behaviors). He was a young man working in a fourth generation family business and expectations for his success as a fourth-generation up-and-comer were high.

He was struggling within his work because he took everything so personally and would become verbally emotional when he was criticized, instructed to do things a certain way or told what to do.

While working with this young man, I offered him the following to consider:

"Emotions do not follow any rules. It is time for you to lead and manage your emotions, rather than letting your emotions lead and manage you."

It was like a light bulb went on for him. "Wow! You're right," he said. "I am allowing my emotions to lead me, rather than the other way around. I need to lead myself, first. This is exactly what I need to do."

From that point on, one of his coaching goals was to manage his emotions when he was feeling stressed from criticism by others or pressed by differing opinions in what he should do. He became more mindful of when he felt strong about a particular subject or was told to do things a certain way. He began to manage his own feelings when he saw that he had a lot on the line to lose.

He did this first by managing the paradigm behind his views on conflict. He realized when faced with differing opinions, it was okay to take a different view. He realized he could feel strongly about a subject, and if someone else felt strongly about a subject, it was okay to not take it personally. Managing his emotions involved changing his thinking about how he felt internally (a lack of self-confidence) and about how he needed to respond (with confidence).

The more he managed his emotions and knew the source of what triggered them, the better he was able to calm his internal and reactive responses. He realized he could bring reason into the process and respond with a clear and level head. His process helped him find his voice – it was okay to disagree with others. And his input began to bring greater value when creatively solving problems and conflicts, since he was not driven by how he "felt," but by the outcome he wanted. He found people were more respectful of him and engaged with him because he was using more thoughtful information, rather than his own feelings about a particular subject. He realized not everything was about him and his emotions. He did not need to be overly sensitive and take things so personally as most things were not about him as much as they were about, "this is how we've always done things from one generation to the next and we're not interested in change." He realized there could be mutual agreement on wanting a good solution for the problem with many different approaches in reaching a good solution.

When our coaching process and time frame of engagement came to a close, I later received a very nice e-mail from this young man thanking me for helping him to overcome his greatest obstacle – his emotions. With his new paradigm, practice and approach to challenging situations, rather than becoming a person who was defeated when things got hard, he became an overcomer and created solutions to make things better. As his coach, I am very proud of the process he created for building greater self-awareness, and of who he has become: a leader who manages his thoughts and behaviors very well. He has not become emotionless as much as he has become a leader of his own emotions, able to appropriately empathize and lead others well creatively.

CREATIVITY
Overcome Obstacles

Today – Focus on being a conqueror of obstacles:
<u>Look for ways to –</u>

- Be a problem solver
- Remove hindrances that stand in your way
- Overcome in spite of the odds against you

<u>Read the above at least three times today.</u>
What do the statements mean to you?

_____

_____

How will you incorporate their meaning into your daily interactions with others?

_____

WEEK 3 / FRIDAY

CONFIDENCE
Stretch Above and Beyond Minimum Expectations

A person who possesses confidence personally and professionally builds trust with others. The quality of their communication is high, and they excel when resolving conflicts. They are able to influence others through listening, gathering feedback, and collaborating with others to find solutions for best results. Confidence is fully realized through the development of the first four C's.

A Review of Your Learning:
Reflect on how you have been able to stretch above and beyond minimum expectations? Write your thoughts below:

- **Admitting mistakes and failures - Character**

  _____
  _____
  _____
  _____

- **Prioritizing your time - Competence**

  _____
  _____
  _____
  _____

- **Keeping commitments - Consistency**

  _____
  _____
  _____
  _____

- **Overcoming obstacles - Creativity**

  _____
  _____
  _____
  _____

After thinking about these areas in which you've discovered stretching above and beyond minimum expectations, how confident do you feel?

_____

_____

_____

_____

"Inaction breeds doubt and fear. Action breeds confidence and courage.
If you want to conquer fear, do not sit home and think about it.
Go out and get busy."
DALE CARNEGIE

CONFIDENCE
Stretch Above and Beyond Minimum Expectations

Today – Focus on the past four days as you have built your CONFIDENCE:
<u>Review how you have learned to –</u>

- **Admit responsibility for failures and mistakes**
- **Prioritize and manage your time**
- **Keep commitments**
- **Overcome obstacles**

<u>Read the above at least three times today.</u>
What do the statements mean to you?

_____
_____

How will you incorporate their meaning into your daily interactions with others?

_____

WEEK 4 / MONDAY

CHARACTER
Respond to Constructive Criticism and Feedback

A person of character knows who they are and why they do what they do. They are able to build trust with others through their integrity, trustworthiness, and honesty.

"The bigger problem was that …
I couldn't see that I had a problem."
"Leadership and Self-Deception"
The Arbinger Institute

In the book "Leadership and Self-Deception," the authors write about a new employee, Tom Callum, at the Zagrum Company. After several weeks with the company, Tom is assigned a leadership mentor. The objective of their relationship is to correct some early management and leadership errors Tom has made. In their first meeting, Tom's mentor states, "Tom, you have a problem. If you are going to have a chance in making an impact in your job, you are going to have to solve your problem."

Have these words been spoken to you, "_____, you have a problem…"? If so, you may have or have had no clue as to what your "problem" was or is.

The reality is, others can see "you have a problem", whether you see it or not. It is possible what others see in you, is what Tom's mentor saw in him, an inability to:

- Respond respectfully to all those who work at the company, regardless of their perceived high or low positions.
- Acknowledge people as people first (not as objects to get work done).
- Perform the functions of his job without blaming others (taking more personal responsibility for mistakes).

Whether at work or at home, it is possible to focus on the *functions* of getting work done while ignoring those who are there to support you, help you, and facilitate completion of work and projects.

Your view of yourself and others matters when interacting with them. Your paradigm will affect your communication style and render you effective or ineffective, approachable or unapproachable and adaptable or inflexible, whether you are at home or in your workplace.

To be effective and successful in leading yourself well, let's look at the reality of leadership weaknesses and strengths.

1) Is your leadership more interested and invested in getting work done? Are you aware of how others are affected by your focus on work alone? Does your focus keep others from providing support to you? Are you aware that your words are constantly telling people what to do rather than allowing them to contribute to helping you solve problems.
   - Is this "problem" in you?

Solution:
It takes self-awareness to understand you play a role and affect others when you are doing your job and communicating with them.

Realize that there is work that requires your expertise and work that will benefit from allowing others to support you and help you get work done. Gathering input from others can help you solve issues and problems together, rather than you solving them alone.

- If, this is not a problem for you, write down what is working well for you?

_____
_____
_____

2) As a leader, do you lack self-awareness? Are you aware that your approach to getting things done is negatively affecting others around you? Is your narrow focus contributing to you ignoring general kindness and not expressing appreciation for others? Are you able to recognize the work that others are contributing?

- Does this "lack of awareness problem" reside in you, too?

Solution:
It takes mindful awareness to see signs from others that indicate they need your focus, appreciation, and general thoughtfulness.

- If, this is not a problem for you, write down what is working well for you?

_____
_____
_____

3) When leading yourself, do you need to pay attention to your own responses and how they are affecting the way others view you? Are others drawing the conclusion that you work for the benefit of yourself and not the organization? Ultimately, do others see you as loyal to the company or having its best interests in mind?

- Do you need to pay attention?

Solution:
It requires slowing down, understanding cues and responses from others, and monitoring your own behavior to build trust and confidence with others.

There is a difference in mindset when working for the good of the organization vs. working for the good of oneself. You will build credibility when others believe you are working for the good of the whole – which includes them.

- If, this is not a problem for you, write down what is working well for you?

_____
_____
_____

4) As you lead, do you respect others? Do you quickly enter into a blame mode when communicating to others? Are you able to stop and ask yourself, "Did I communicate effectively with the person to obtain a mutual understanding of each of our needs and expectations?"
   - Does your communication style need improvement?

Solution:
Communicating clearly is key. Being mindful of the words you speak and the responses you give to others will give you greater insight into the situation and the other person.
   - If, this is not a problem for you, write down what is working well for you?

_____

_____

_____

5) Is your leadership style flexible and able to adjust in different cultures? Do you expect everyone around you to adapt to your style and your approach, rather than considering what others need from you?
   - Are you unapproachable and unable to adapt to new cultures and new ways of doing things?

Solution:
Leadership is a commitment to making personal adjustments within the context of the situation, finding solutions to problems, and resolving conflict.
   - If, this is not a problem for you, write down what is working well for you?

_____

_____

_____

Communication is key to everything you do and to your success as a leader. When you are willing to be open to constructive criticism and feedback, along with making adjustments to grow with productive, helpful, and useful critiques, you will progress in your work and personal life.

When you are focused on the big picture of leading yourself well and receiving feedback from others, you will grow in self-awareness and self-management of your behavior. You have the choice to be:

- A problem
  or
- A part of the solution

- Lacking in self-awareness
  or
- Willing to seek greater clarity

- An avoider
  or

- Attentive to situations

- Resentful
  or
- A mindful communicator with best intentions

- Stuck
  or
- Adaptable, with the best interests of all in mind

You always have a choice among paradigms. Ultimately, it is in your best interest to get feedback. Feedback and constructive criticism have the potential to help you build self-confidence, humility, and skill in handling challenging situations. All you need do is be open to and listen to them.

As we look back at our fictional character Tom, "who had a problem", he was self-deceived by a lack of self-awareness, self-management and the inability to ask for constructive feedback. The constructive feedback did come to him. And, it came through his leadership mentors last attempt to use corrective measures before he was fired. Did Tom learn to change and adapt to his new culture? You'll need to read, "Leadership and Self-Deception" as we do not want to give away the ending.

We encourage you to ask for constructive feedback with those who are helpful and want the best for you. We are not saying that you must receive and respond to all criticism and feedback. We are saying that every piece of good and healthy feedback will help you raise the bar of your performance.

Three things create remarkable success when you seek feedback:

- People will feel more comfortable speaking their minds around you.
- People will know that you are pursuing excellence.
- People will admire your openness and willingness to respond to helpful and healthy feedback.

CHARACTER
Respond to Constructive Criticism and Feedback

Today – Focus on your response to:

- **Unsolicited advice**
- **Productive critique**
- **Helpful analysis**
- **Useful views**

<u>Read the above at least three times today.</u>
What do the statements mean to you?

_____

_____

How will you incorporate their meaning into your daily interactions with others?

_____

WEEK 4 / TUESDAY

COMPETENCE
Act When You See an Opportunity

A person of competence understands the reality of their skills and knows how they bring value to their relationships and work with their expertise. They are able to build trust with others through their well-known capabilities, qualifications, and experiences.

"What got you here, won't get you there!"
MARSHALL GOLDSMITH

Our thoughts are with you as you embrace the path to leadership success. Your intentional and positive choices will get you to where you want to go and who you want to be as part of the marginal gains mindset. And yet, there is more for your present choices to influence your future desired outcomes. Are you curious? Your leadership success requires an action plan.

Think about the following statements:

- All opportunities are formed through people you know.
- All opportunities come through constantly expanding your network.
- All opportunities exist as you seek the correct relationships with people who recommend you and endorse you.

What is an opportunity that came through a person you know?

_____
_____
_____

Our experience is this:

- Opportunities do not appear out of thin air.
- Dreams do not come true out of nowhere.
- Relationships do not form without our focused effort and interactions.

**"The future does not get better by hope;
it gets better by plan."**
JIM ROHN, ENTREPRENEUR

What motivates you to meet new people?

_____
_____
_____

To act when you see an opportunity is to be open to meeting new people. As you constantly place yourself in new situations, new people are available to you anywhere and everywhere you go.

> **"Opportunities aren't so much found as they are created. You create the possibility for opportunity every time you say 'yes' to a request."**
> PAUL HUDSON

Tess Goes to the Hospital

In 2008, I was asked to coach a large group of medical professionals. My only prior experiences with the medical profession were as a patient and taking my children to their pediatrician for checkups. Professionally, I did not have a lot of experience; yet, as an executive coach, I was willing to enter into a new culture of work at this hospital. So, I seized the opportunity for a new professional experience and accepted the offer.

Was I nervous to be in a new professional environment? You bet.

Was I concerned that I did not have all of the skills that I needed to enter into such complex coaching relationships? Absolutely.

Just like everyone else, health care professionals are people first, and I realized that with my expertise in coaching and my proven processes for coaching, I was prepared, capable, and able to meet the expectations and demands of this new opportunity.

What I found interesting about my own self-awareness and thought process was this: My confidence increased after I knew my "why" for accepting the role. I said, "Yes" because I wanted to continue to grow and develop as a professional executive coach within an industry I had yet to experience. My work with medical professionals was a tremendous privilege. The most rewarding aspect was helping to improve their quality of communication both with one another and their patients. This, in turn, benefited both the patients and the hospital administration.

When I said "Yes" to myself, to new relationships, to new opportunities, and to new ways of seeing my own contributions as being helpful in a new professional environment, I began to unfold a whole new world that also gave me a firmer foundation for saying "Yes" to future opportunities and relationships. May the same be true for you.

Dan Finds the Urgency of Urgency

My career in sales training provides many opportunities to practice useful strategies. The most important quality for salespeople in my industry is a sense of urgency about meeting new people. When they meet new and potential client's they begin to gather the necessary information we need to build a positive relationship.

We sell a relatively commoditized group of products, so our only major differentiators from competitors are:

- Our ability to connect with those we meet
- Our excellent service

- Our accuracy and attention to detail
- Our speed in delivery

If a salesperson lacks urgency in any of these areas, the dozens of little things he encounters on a daily basis pile up rapidly. If he does not take care of this growing list, over a short period – say, within two days – his to-do list can swell to 20-30 items that need his attention immediately.

As the to-do list grows out of control, paralysis sets in because the mountain of tedious, albeit necessary, work becomes nearly insurmountable. Because not taking care of these things finally causes enough pain, he ultimately diverts focus to these tedious tasks, which causes him to stop meeting new people. The downward spiral is almost out of control by this point.

We've established that selling is a numbers game. When a salesperson diverts his attention to "non-selling" activities (such as returning non-urgent phone calls, emails, text messages, and loitering on social media), he actively breaks the rules of the numbers game and loses sight of the activities that are truly important:

- Prospecting for new opportunities
- Maintaining projects
- Planning for the future
- Building relationships

When focused attention turns to a true sense of urgency as your way of doing things and making decisions, you will be in the minority of the population. And you will seem to accomplish more than the average person thinks is possible.

We suggest keeping the following two thoughts a high priority:

- Be capable, demonstrating an ability to get things done.
- Make meeting new people your priority.

Consistently doing these two things will create a surplus of new opportunities for you.

Take these next steps to help you.

1) Get things done in a timely manner so you are free to meet new people.

What time-management strategy do you need to implement in getting things done? You will need to eliminate something from your current daily schedule, if you choose to make meeting new people a priority. What will that be?

_____

_____

What is the level of urgency that you need to meet new people? Is it strong or not so important to you?

_____

_____

Set a date for implementing your new strategy: _____

_____

2) Create a new opportunity. Envision a new opportunity that you would like to say, "yes" to, and write it down. How urgent is creating this new opportunity to you?

_____

_____

_____

_____

_____

Set a date by which you would like to experience this new opportunity:

_____

3) Are you doing the necessary things to create and enter into your desired new opportunity?

_____

What would help you do the necessary things? What new habits should you develop to embrace your new opportunity?

Write down three steps you need to take:
1)_____

_____

2)_____

_____

3)_____

_____

Note: If you visit our website, **www.theleadershipblueprint.com** our coaches will assist you in creating a new strategy.

COMPETENCE
Act When You See an Opportunity

Today – Focus on your personal and professional performance:
<u>Take advantage of –</u>

- **Joining others for greater impact**
  Meet someone new.

- **Seeking out one thing that helps you to perform at a higher level**
  Assess the risk and reward gained by taking action.

- **Saying yes and acting**
  Take a leap of faith.

<u>Read the above at least three times today.</u>
What do the statements mean to you?

_____

_____

How will you incorporate their meaning into your daily interactions with others?

_____

WEEK 4 / WEDNESDAY

CONSISTENCY
Practice, Practice, and Practice Some More

A consistent person is known for being reliable. They are able to build trust with others by creating predictable structures, systems, and measurable results. They also have the ability to stabilize situations.

> **"Success is the sum of small efforts,**
> **repeated day in and day out."**
> ROBERT COLLIER
> AMERICAN AUTHOR OF SELF-HELP BOOKS

On January 15, 2009, Capt. Chesley B. "Sully" Sullenberger made an emergency landing of US Airways Flight 1549 in New York's Hudson River. One hundred fifty passengers and five crew members were on board. Due to Sullenberger's quick action, everyone survived. The event became known as the "Miracle on the Hudson."

During the initial take off and climb out, the plane struck a flock of Canadian geese and immediately lost engine power. There was no time to return to the airport. Sully decided to land in the river. The entire crew was awarded the Master's Medal by the Guild of Air Pilots and Air Navigators. This event exemplified the highest level of true heroics: amazing intellect, skill, confidence, and courage. Most importantly, it revealed Sully's true mastery in two areas: the ability to operate with calm under pressure, and the ability to land a plane in a river… he could have landed the plane almost anywhere!

How did he do it?

Sullenberger was a former fighter pilot who had been a commercial airline pilot since he left the U.S. Air Force in 1980. Sullenberger had logged 19,664 flight hours, 4,765 of which were accumulated in Airbust A320 aircraft, the type of plane he piloted on January 15, 2009.

He possessed practice and preparation.

Listen to the US Airways flight 1549 full cockpit recording on YouTube and note Sully's calm demeanor. Multiple airports are discussed as emergency landing options, and Sully rejects them all as the full measure of his predicament becomes clear. When an air traffic controller asks him which runway he would like to use, he calmly replies, "We can't do it. We're going to be in the Hudson." The most incredible part of the recording is not the words themselves, but the casual nature and extreme focus Sullenberger possessed in the moment. The air traffic controllers go on to discuss other runway availability, and finally one of them says, "I think he said he's in the Hudson."

To watch and listen to Sullenberger's mastery, go to
http://www.youtube.com/watch?v=imDFSnklB0k
In Malcolm Gladwell's book, "Outliers," he writes that to attain a level of mastery in a pursuit, statistics indicate that we need to practice appropriate behaviors and action for at least 10,000 hours. Sounds like a lot of hours, right? Almost too overwhelming to begin.

The average human in the Western world lives at least 483,000 waking hours – 17 hours a day for 77.8 years. If you can attain mastery at your life's main pursuit in only 10,000 hours of practice – 2.07 percent of your waking life – isn't the pursuit worth starting?

The path to mastery is a long succession of plateaus, punctuated by spikes of enhanced understanding and ability. Most people don't see the results they want quickly enough, so they tend to abandon their efforts far too early. Ten thousand hours of practice may sound mind-boggling, but most people do not grasp the progression as they work through this amount of time. If you will focus on building your skills, you will make progressive, worthwhile steps along the way.

Most people perceive skill progression in this way:

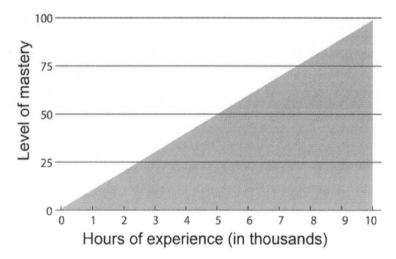

When in fact, *true* skill progression looks more like this:

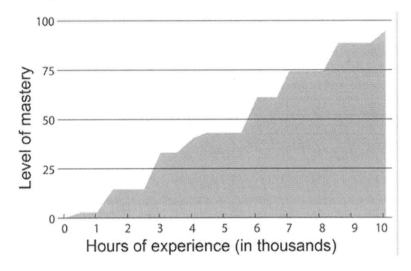

Attaining mastery will require a lot of work. Ask yourself these questions before beginning the journey:

- What do I truly aspire to do with my life?
- Can I do what I aspire to do?
- Is it worth the sacrifice to do what I aspire to do?

If you can answer these questions definitively and affirmatively, you have the beginning necessary motivation to create a plan for practice. If you focus on regular practice, you will find you are committed to consistency, which prepares you to respond to both obstacles and opportunities. Practice, in turn helps you embrace plateaus, generate epiphanies, and exceed your expectations.

Three places to begin your practice:

1) Practice training your mind and thoughts for best outcomes. Yes, you need to train and self-manage what you think. Everything you do begins with a thought. The exercise and preparation in training your thought patterns affects what you do and every outcome you experience.

In your mind, what thoughts need to be trained and practiced to create good outcomes?

_____

_____

_____

_____

_____

_____

_____

_____

_____

2) Practice creates positive habits. Experiences that benefit you and others need to be practiced over and over. Exceptional habits do not just happen in a vacuum. They are well thought out, constructed and planned. (And, the same holds true, if you want to quit a negative habit, you must practice a new, positive habit.)

What new habits will you practice to help you create positive experiences for you and others?

_____
_____
_____
_____
_____
_____
_____
_____

3) All verbal and written communications regarding what you have chosen to do need to be rehearsed. We do not use our best communication when we "wing it." We are most effective when we practice what we want to communicate out loud and in front of a mirror. Your ability to practice your words and structure of thoughts within a sentence allows you to create a smooth and natural flow when communicating with others, which increases your credibility and confidence.

What information do you need to internalize and practice that will inspire people to listen to you and build your trustworthiness when working with others?

_____
_____
_____
_____
_____
_____
_____
_____

The repetition of productive practice means that you can and will get better. Great things happen when you practice and prepare!

> **"History has demonstrated
> that the most notable winners
> usually encountered heartbreaking obstacles
> before they triumphed.
> They won because they refused to
> become discouraged by the defeats."**
> BERTIE CHARLES FORBES
> FOUNDER OF FORBES MAGAZINE

CONSISTENCY
Practice, Practice, and Practice Some More

Today – Focus on repeating good behaviors:
<u>Practice in the following ways –</u>

- Train your thoughts and mind for good outcomes
- Repeat habits that create positive experiences and responses from others
- Rehearse and internalize important information
  Prepare verbal and written exercises to increase best results

<u>Read the above at least three times today.</u>
What do the statements mean to you?

_____

_____

How will you incorporate their meaning into your daily interactions with others?

_____

WEEK 4 / THURSDAY

CREATIVITY
Be a Visionary

An influential person has the ability to create strong relationships and build trust with others. They are able to think of new ideas and process input with others. Their solutions produce excellent outcomes for the good of themselves and others.

> **"Don't fear big.**
> **Fear mediocrity.**
> **Fear waste.**
> **Fear the lack of living to your fullest."**
> GARY KELLER
> AUTHOR OF "THE ONE THING"

Create a vision for your future.
What inspires you to create a vision for your future?

You've heard the terms "big picture," "30,000-foot view," "high-level thinking," and probably several more describing the concept of envisioning for the future. It is possible that this concept of vision is difficult for you to think about, as realistic thinking tends to be the norm for every day living.

Being realistic is foundational to creating a vision and it is the very thing that helps you to build trust with others. As you face your own realities you build confidence that others have in you.

We want you to listen to your own thoughts and find a connection to your ideal future. We're going to call the creation of your vision "Laying out your blueprint." It's you imagining, looking down on the design of what you want your life to look like and, as it will someday be.

A creative vision communicated with clarity by you, as a leader of your own self first, gives you the opportunity to give your followers direction, understanding and a level of security. People need reasons to keep moving forward. *You* need a reason to keep moving forward and leading yourself well. Your personal blueprint is the plan of your future to more fully realize your own talents and strengths. Your blueprint provides you with a compelling list of reasons to explain why you are doing what you are doing, how you are going to do what is necessary, and how to direct your actions toward the outcomes you seek.

Your personal vision blueprint communicated clearly and appropriately will answer the following questions affirmatively:

- "Does what I'm doing have personal meaning?"
  Do I **really** want to do this?

- "Am I making progress toward an outcome?"
  Are the **measurable** results and rewards appropriate?

- "Are my contributions making a difference?"
  Are the final **results** fulfilling?

When you feel that who you are and what you are doing bring value to yourself and others, it becomes a motivator for forward motion. You will find yourself propelled out of bed in the morning. You will work with intensity all day. And you will end your day looking forward to tomorrow. If you do this well, your followers will feel the same way. This is how you build a high-performing life and organization.

Here is a way to keep your momentum going as you create your own leadership blueprint:

Focus on executing your vision and solving problems, which will create clarity for you and others.

To create greater focus and clarity of "who" you are, remind yourself:

- What is most important to me?

  _____

- What am I most passionate about?

  _____

- What energizes me every day?

  _____

- What motivates me to get up every morning?

  _____

When you focus on your true answers to these questions, you will build your capacity to know who you are, why you do what you do in life and work, and how you are going to create a lifetime of meaning for you and others. Your reflection provides the beginning drafts of your leadership blueprint.

In the midst of living your vision you will discover a common theme that creates a desire to live up to your full potential.

In Parts 2 and 3 of this book, you will carefully design strategies for completing your leadership blueprint. You will increase your capacity to survive amidst the complexities and challenges that arise in life and work. You will have the opportunity to develop a "Capt. Sullenburger's" level of calm that will allow you to lead your life with expectation and contribute with the highest level of character, competence, consistency, creativity and confidence.

Your blueprint will be affirmed and reinforced as it influences your behavior and the behavior of others for decades.

Your blueprint will be a commitment that you make to yourself that becomes a guide for your future decisions.

Your blueprint will bring an inner feeling of calm and outward experience of success as you practice and build upon your strengths.

Your blueprint will meet a core need of describing who you are, who you want to be, and how you want to live your life with meaning: your legacy. Your legacy does not begin at the end of your life; it is built by the choices you make every single day of your life and career.

Your blueprint is vitally important. As Gary Keller states, "What you build today will either empower or restrict your tomorrow."

Remember, vision takes time and preparation.

It's time for you to focus on you, your present reality, and your future hope.

It's time to set goals and strategies, the foundation for all of your success.

> **"Who shall set a limit to the influence
> of a human being?"**
> RALPH WALDO EMERSON

Preparation In Designing Your Blueprint

In the exercise below, think about each area in its prime. What would each area look like for you as it grows in importance? We are not saying look at each area in its perfection, but in the ways in which it can be its best.

Begin by writing a brief vision statement for each focus below:

- **Your personal life**

  _____
  _____
  _____

- **Your family life**

  _____
  _____
  _____

- **Your friendships in life**

  _____
  _____
  _____

- **Your professional life**

  _____
  _____
  _____

- **Your monetary life**

  _____
  _____
  _____

- **Your physical life**

  _____
  _____
  _____

- **Your spiritual life**

  _____
  _____
  _____

- **Your desired legacy**

  _____
  _____
  _____

"You are never too old to set another goal or to dream a new dream."
C.S. LEWIS

"Twenty years from now you will be more disappointed by the things
you didn't do than by the ones you did do. So throw off the bowlines.
Sail away from the safe harbor. Catch the trade winds in your sail.
Explore. Dream. Discover."
MARK TWAIN

CREATIVITY
BE A VISIONARY

Today – Focus on the possibilities for the future:
> <u>We encourage you to –</u>

- Create a vision for yourself
- Engage visionary people around you who are idealistic and creative
- Develop a clear understanding of your reality and your hopes for creating a future

<u>Read the above at least three times today.</u>
What do the statements mean to you?

_____

_____

How will you incorporate their meaning into your daily interactions with others?

_____

WEEK 4 / FRIDAY

CONFIDENCE
Influence

A person who possesses confidence personally and professionally builds trust with others. The quality of their communication is high, and they excel when resolving conflicts. They are able to influence others through listening, gathering feedback, and collaborating with others to find solutions for best results. Confidence is fully realized through the development of the first four C's.

A Review of Your Learning:
Reflect on how you have been able to influence your own habits in the areas mentioned above? Write your thoughts below:

- **Responding to feedback - Character**

  _____
  _____
  _____
  _____

- **Taking action - Competence**

  _____
  _____
  _____
  _____

- **Practicing - Consistency**

  _____
  _____
  _____
  _____

- **Being a person of vision - Creativity**

  _____
  _____
  _____
  _____

After thinking about these areas in which you've discovered ways to influence your own behaviors first, how confident do you feel?

_____
_____
_____

You are the architect of leading and living your best life.

"I am not a product of my circumstances. I am a product of my decisions."
STEPHEN COVEY

At this point in the book, you can feel confident in staying true to who you are due to your commitment to your personal growth and development. Your experience as a learner has required thoughtful, hard work on your part and we recognize and affirm your efforts.

You have successfully completed Part 1 of your self-directed leadership and learning journey. The knowledge you have acquired and the reflection in which you have engaged while processing your thoughts and opinions are now part of who you are – part of your leadership story.

Your personal and professional transformation is just beginning … there is more ahead for you to learn, invest in and grow as you continue to create your leadership blueprint. Keep envisioning more for your life, personally and professionally. Your leadership will continue to move forward as you create a strategy of focus for your leadership. We value your commitment as you move forward in Parts 2, 3 and 4.

TESS COX AND DANIEL KLAWER

CONFIDENCE
Influence

Today – Focus on the past four days as you have built your confidence through mastering the art of leadership influence:

<u>Note how you have learned to –</u>

Respond to constructive criticism and feedback
Act when you see an opportunity
Practice ... practice ... practice ...
Be a visionary

<u>Read the above at least three times today.</u>
What do the statements mean to you?

_____

_____

How will you incorporate their meaning into your daily interactions with others?

_____

PART 2

DESIGNING YOUR LEADERSHIP BLUEPRINT

"Before you are a leader, success is all about growing yourself.
When you become a leader, success is all about the growth of others."
JACK WELCH

HOW TO READ PART 2 OF THIS BOOK

art 1 provided you with daily readings to increase your self-understanding and professional development. You focused on building your self-awareness with the 5 C's of Leadership – Character, Competence, Consistency, Creativity, and Confidence. The stories, coaching reflections, and questions afforded you the opportunity to think seriously about leading yourself well when living and working with others. Throughout the daily readings, you learned that you are the leader of your own self, first. And, you learned, your life is built upon your choices, layer upon layer, every minute of every day. You decide who you are going to be, how you are going to respond to challenges, and what really matters most to you. You are the leader and the architect of your life and work. Your commitment to your leadership gives you the opportunity to create meaning and purpose with every choice you make and in everything you do.

Part 2 is a new commitment to your pursuit of personal self-understanding and professional development. The next four-week focus raises the bar for you and builds on your learning from Part 1. At the beginning of each new week, we will choose a focus statement for you from the first four of the 5 C's of Leadership: Character, Competence, Consistency, and Creativity (in Part 3 we will focus on building your leadership blueprint for Confidence). Also, we will guide you to develop a new paradigm with a focus statement. You will learn to create a support statement and strategy to reach your desired outcomes using your new paradigm and focus. Every week you will have the opportunity to practice key elements of your strategy – we call them "habits of choice."

At the end of your four-week learning and new-strategy implementation, you will have developed new leadership skills in leading yourself every day in the following ways:

- **The way you think** about how you use your intellect and see yourself with a new mindset or paradigm.
- **The way you process information** and use the strengths of who you are to create a new strategy that reflects your new attitudes and behaviors.
- **The way you develop new skills** in understanding where you want to go with your new leadership, skills and expertise.
- **The way you order your world** by using developed, positive, and affirming habits.
- **The way you engage with others** by using your emotional self-understanding to build meaningful relationships with others.

In Part 1, we used the model on the next page to introduce you to the concept of leading yourself well with the process of considering the way you think, process information, develop skills, order your world and engage with others. In Part 2, we ask you to use the model as a guide to create your new strategies, which will help you lead yourself well. Your new strategies will create the effective leadership you want to experience and construct the life you want to live.

This four-week focus requires a larger time commitment than Part 1. We suggest scheduling at least 60 minutes per week for your self-directed learning experience. This will give you the appropriate amount of time to read, learn, and create your daily strategies, and it will give you a reminder to practice what you have learned.

THINK

ENGAGE
WITH OTHERS

PROCESS
INFORMATION

ORDER
YOUR WORLD

DEVELOP
SKILLS

> **"The key to learning from success is to pause and take the time to understand what's working…Moving beyond a hunch to actual data and analysis can be enlightening and empowering."**
> ROGER CONNORS AND TOM SMITH –
> AUTHORS OF FIXIT – GETTING ACCOUNTABILITY RIGHT

Leaders who are the architects of their personal and professional lives choose to build self-awareness, which is a continued understanding of their emotional strengths and weaknesses. When a leader is able to identify the "why" of their emotional responses to others who are different from themselves and manage their emotions with confidence and competence, they think in the following ways:

1) First and foremost, I am the leader of myself before I can lead anyone else.
2) The foundation for leading my own life begins with my Character.
3) In order to lead my life with excellence, the pillars that support my leadership are Competence, Consistency, and Creativity.
4) The three areas that will build my Confidence are a focus on self-awareness of who I am today, who I want to become, and the way I self-manage my behavior.
5) I am able to influence others and lead my life well through appropriate self-reflection and strategies, which will increase my leadership capacity.

We know this to be true about paradigms and strategies:

- Your thoughts alone will not create the outcomes of who you want to be.
- You need new thoughts, new attitudes, and new behaviors to become the person you envision.
- A well-developed and mindful strategy to lead your life and career is a critical prelude to experiencing your goals and desired outcomes.

In order to experience new and different outcomes in your life and work, you need a strategic leadership blueprint.

In Part 1, we introduced the concept of marginal gains. Over a period of time, a strategy of attaining marginal gains will help you replace your old habits with new habits. As you practice these new habits, you will begin to experience a transformational change that will give you increased energy to continue working and become the person you desire to be and do the things that are important to you.

In Part 2, as you create a leadership blueprint for your life and work, you will increase in your leadership effectiveness. You will be mindful of your everyday choices as they propel the forward motion of your marginal gains. With a focus on increasing your leadership effectiveness and as you practice your new and helpful strategies - you will be encouraged to reflect on the transformational change taking place within you and beginning to influence your external outcomes.

Transformational change (converting your thoughts and energy into something new) begins when you acknowledge your need for an internal change. This is your starting point, as you choose to create a new paradigm and blueprint for that change. You will learn to lead yourself with a focus on the positive and make good choices for your benefit and the well being of others.

Strategies vs. Shortcuts – Reflection From Tess

Within the coaching context, incremental steps, clear strategies, and consistent practice are keys to building a new memory bank of behaviors. Some clients have said to me, "Tess, just tell me what I need to change, and I'll do it." They want me to tell them what to do.

Telling others what to do and how to do things is appropriate for some situations, but learning to be a better leader of yourself is not one of them. Clients who want to be told what to change and do are really saying to me, "Tess, I do not want to take the time to be reflective and create an effective strategy to do things differently. My productivity in my work is too important for me to be able to pause and reflect on my own leadership effectiveness. I've got too much work to do and I am too busy. Since you are my coach, *you* be reflective for me – tell me what I need to change and create the strategy for me." Unfortunately, clients with this mindset do not see reflection and creating their own strategy as productive or necessary in leading themselves well, and they want a shortcut.

There is a problem with shortcuts. Shortcuts do not provide the much-needed reflection for internalization and strategy that leads to transformational change. A shortcut might work as a band-aid in the moment, but it won't bring added value and benefits down the road when a behavioral mindset change is needed to problem solve and make decisions. There are no internalized memories trained for the new behavior. Shortcuts will not prepare a leader for more complex problem solving or the need to make collective strategic decisions. Old mindsets and behaviors are not sustainable nor will they produce new positive outcomes.

What is wrong with merely telling you what you should do, think, or change?

1) You will not see or understand your current reality. You may often think someone else has created your current situation, which may lead you to an unwillingness to be fully responsible for your life and work.

2) If you cannot see your current reality and the changes you need to make for yourself, you will not take personal ownership of your own thoughts, attitudes, and behaviors. You may be unwilling to be fully responsible for your life and work.

3) If you are waiting to be told what to do, how to think, and what to change, you will not know how to create your own new thoughts, attitudes, and behaviors for healthy change. You might blame others when things do not go as planned.

4) If you have not developed the necessary skills to create the new paradigms, strategies, and practices for positive change and forward motion, the best of outcomes may never be attained. You will be tempted to blame others and simply say, "I can't change." You will have a mindset of unwillingness to be fully responsible for your life and work.

As a leader, being fully responsible for your life and work is a personal and professional acceptance of and openness to change.

TESS COX AND DANIEL KLAWER

Within the coaching engagement, Tess guides leaders to be fully responsible for their paradigms, strategies, and practices for positive change. She is able to guide a client to, and through, the steps of transformational change. How does this work? It starts with a focus on a new paradigm, strategy, and practice. She cannot create a new paradigm and workable strategy for her clients or make them practice them. But she can hold them accountable for doing what they say they want to do. Every client has to do the necessary internal reflection for their own transformational change, which, in turn, begins to alter their external experiences and increases their knowledge, depth of insight, and understanding of themselves.

There is a simple truth in life with the 5 C's of Leadership (Character, Competence, Consistency, Creativity, and Confidence) in mind: The pace of self-directed learning is up to you. Regardless of your pace and comfort level, we encourage you to stay committed to your personal learning, growth, and development. Why? Because *the way you lead yourself today matters for where you will find yourself tomorrow.* Your leadership requires that you reflect on and practice your own strategies for life and work.

We have designed a process that will encourage you to gather constructive feedback from others. We ask you to engage those closest to you in the process. It will be helpful for you to know and understand how others perceive you as you move forward. We encourage you to be honest with yourself and transparent with others. Ask them to do the same with you.

Your willingness to change, grow, and develop may feel uncomfortable at first, and yet, being able to ask for and act on feedback from others as an independent and committed learner is the most important factor in achieving good, healthy, and transformational change.

WEEK ONE

DESIGNING YOUR CHARACTER BLUEPRINT

Take your personal and professional temperature on CHARACTER:
On a scale of 1 to 5 (1 being low and 5 being high), how do you rate the way you lead your life with Character?

Do you see a difference in how you scored yourself from last month?
To refresh your memory, look at page 11.

Describe any changes you've seen as you've focused on building your Character:

_____

_____

Is transformational change in your character needed in your life, family, or career?
Explain your thoughts:

_____

_____

_____

_____

Key words for building your CHARACTER strategy

Trust
Credibility
Responsibility
Well-reasoned responses

Synopsis of the daily "Character focus" from every Monday in Part 1:

- Your Character builds trust with others. When you are known as a person of integrity, others will trust your intent, actions, words, and outcomes.
- As a person of Character, you are able to build your credibility with others. When you have credibility, you raise the bar of excellence for others and yourself.
- As a person who strives to maintain credibility and excellent Character, you are able to accept responsibility for failures and mistakes. You are able to see your failures or mistakes as personal and professional growth opportunities.
- As a person of Character, you are able to respond to constructive criticism and feedback. You seek new solutions to problems and find new ways of dealing with critical issues. You move from being an individual contributor to being a leader who is able to embrace the input and opinions of others.

A person of character knows who they are and why they do what they do. They are able to build trust with others through their integrity, trustworthiness, and honesty.

COACHING QUESTION

Ask three close family members or peers if they find you trustworthy, and why or why not.
   Record their responses:

1)
_____
_____

2)
_____
_____

3)
_____
_____

The practice of integrity and being a person who is honest, trustworthy, truthful, and reliable is a worthy goal for everyone. Think of someone you know who exemplifies this essential *Character* foundation of integrity.

What are their key behaviors?
_____
_____
_____
_____

What specific qualities within those behaviors do you value with regard to their Character?
_____
_____
_____
_____

The familiar saying is true: Honesty is the best policy. Remember the movie "Catch Me If You Can?" Frank Abagnale wasn't honest. He chose to rationalize his behavior. His Character was compromised by his "little white lies" that shaded the facts and covered up the details. Before he knew it, he was buried in lies and self-deception. Every day he had a choice to begin with a new paradigm, attitude, and behaviors, yet he chose quite the opposite as he continued to live his life of crime and deception.

   Every day you have a choice to be seen as someone who can be trusted, who has high integrity, and who is honest and truthful, someone others can believe in.

With a focus on you and your leadership, what are your thoughts regarding the phrase, "someone others can believe in"?

_____
_____
_____
_____
_____
_____
_____

Tess' Experience With Healthy Work Environments

It is always a privilege to coach accomplished members of the medical community. One of the key elements of their success is their dedication to putting their patients' care first. The high standards of providing quality patient care day in and day out are implemented through a commitment to strategy. Standardized processes are created to ensure the highest quality of teamwork. As a result of high standards and processes, staff and patients experience a "culture of Character," which builds mutual trust between staff and patients and permeates the surrounding community.

In hospitals, the quality of care is not just about high intellect and skill. Every hospital has a set of core values, which may include listening to patients, using the human touch and appropriate empathy, and making decisions that will work toward the best outcome according to the patients' needs. We call this a culture that is rich in intellect and high in emotional intelligence when working on behalf of the good of others. Everything and everyone in a hospital affects the quality and sustainability of patient care. The quality of standardized and strategic care is the essence of character and competence working together within the hospital culture. This type of hospital culture creates an environment of consistency and healthy relationships.

A Young Physician Builds Her Character

People think of doctors as experts in personal health care. It's probable that they do not think of them as business leaders or managers of people. In reality, this type of leadership relationship exists and is more important than any leadership relationship you would find in any business throughout the world. The leadership relationships doctors create and maintain are a matter of life and death.

I had an opportunity to work with a young doctor (we'll call her Dr. Jane) who was on the verge of being dismissed due to her inability to work with her office staff and nurses. Dr. Jane's character was ethical when involving patient care but flawed in her approach to working with her staff. I was hired to help her realize that she was the problem between her and her staff and to help her identify ways to change her thoughts and behaviors when working with her team.

As we began to build our working relationship, Dr. Jane said to me, "Tess, I've been trained to listen and empathize on behalf of my patients. I know when I walk into my patient's exam room that they have my complete attention, focus, and care. I have not been trained to listen and empathize on behalf of my office staff and nurses. I simply have no patience for any of them." To be fair to her professors, it is possible that Dr. Jane "missed" the teaching that trained her how to work well with her office staff and nurses.

We had a lot of work to do with her mindset and current behaviors toward her staff. Keeping her job depended on how well she could make a transformational change in her Character. Dr. Jane needed her staff to trust her; she needed to raise the bar of her own behavior; she needed to look for new ways of communicating with her staff; and she needed to respond to constructive feedback appropriately. She needed a new paradigm focus, a mindset that would support that new paradigm, and a new strategy for practicing new behaviors. Her "habits of choice" would begin to help her to remember how to react and respond appropriately to her staff in all situations.

We began with Dr. Jane's backstory to help us understand the problem we needed to solve:

As I listened to Dr. Jane's story, the root problem became very clear. We both came to the conclusion that her problem was rooted in her Character:

- Dr. Jane's personal story reflected a flaw in her upbringing in learning to show respect for others and receiving respect for herself.
- She did not see her staff as human beings; she saw them as objects to serve her.
- Dr. Jane did not recognize that her staff members were well trained and wanted to do their best work.
- She saw her staff through a distorted view that hindered her ability to communicate effectively with them.
- Dr. Jane found building trust with her patients an important part of her providing the best patient care.
- She realized her struggle to build trust with her staff was ultimately hurting her ability to give her patients the highest quality of care.
- She was emotionally moved to realize her poor relationships with her staff were not serving her patients well.

Foundational character statement for Dr. Jane:
Be trustworthy, a person who cares about others.

Building her mindset

Dr. Jane needed to change her paradigm about her staff. She needed to raise the bar for herself and implement new competencies within her character by "being trustworthy and caring about others – *all others.*"

Building Dr. Jane's habits of practice:

1) Through instrumental assessments that helped us examine her personality traits, handling conflict, and leadership qualities, Dr. Jane realized that she needed to lead her staff with a higher level of understanding her staff and clarity in her communication. Her ability to communicate her best intentions when communicating with others would serve her well.
2) She began to grasp a deeper understanding of how good, healthy leadership includes appropriate care for and interest in the well-being of her staff.
3) She began responding with care and interest towards her staff, which in turn increased positive responses and care from them toward her.

Next, we looked at the reality of her patient-care schedule and office time. We were able to identify specific, critical gaps in her office time, which gave us the opportunity to prioritize how she spent her time in the office when she was not seeing patients.

We created a support strategy for her focus:

1) Together, we *prioritized* her office time.
2) We kept a strict *schedule* for updating charts.
3) We identified specific people with whom she needed to improve her *communication*.
4) We scheduled daily one-on-one time for 5-10 minutes with a certain staff member or members to communicate clarity and understanding (depending on the importance of the issues).
5) We identified a once-a-week *lunch* hour that she could spend eating with staff or checking in with them.
6) I encouraged Dr. Jane to *interact* intentionally and authentically with her nurses and staff for at least 5-10 minutes before she began seeing patients for the day. This gave her an opportunity to connect with them and set the tone for each new day. Yes, it did mean that she had to arrive 5-10 minutes earlier, but the results in building her relationships with them were worth the investment in time.

We reviewed her habits of choice and highlighted key words (demonstrated above).

In order for Dr. Jane to remember her habits of choice, we highlighted important words for her to remember:

- Prioritize
- Schedule
- Communicate

- One-on-one
- Lunch
- Interact

As Dr. Jane remembered these six words, they reminded her to implement her new habits and behaviors.

The positive outcomes:

- Dr. Jane's new ways of seeing her staff as smart, capable and doing their best, yet at times, imperfect (her paradigm shift, rather than seeing them not as smart as she, not as capable as she and not doing their best like she) and her new ways of interacting and communicating with her team increased her integrity and built trust with them.
- She experienced a new confidence in her leadership approach due to her responsible and reliable behavior. The entire team began to act more professionally.
- Dr. Jane realized that being open and responsive to constructive feedback made a better doctor and an improved leader of her own self, her staff, and her patients. Patients began to notice how well everyone was communicating and getting along, which made them feel safe and well-cared-for.
- Her habits of choice reminded her to keep her strategy in mind every day, and she found her new habits worked, which made her happier, too.

As Dr. Jane continued to implement her character focus, new paradigm, strategy, and practice, she found a new willingness to receive feedback and constructive criticism from her staff. The office culture began to change, and the overall experience became a win-win-win for doctor, patients, and staff. To believe that it all began with a focus statement – a focus on Character.

Sample Blueprint for Building Your Leadership Through Your Character
Before you begin this exercise, read the following sample blueprint in its completed form.
You can refer back to this completed sample when building your own blueprint for your Character.

WEEK 1 - CHARACTER
Building your blueprint for your character

Stage 1.	**Character statement**
	Integrity builds trust with others.
Stage 2.	**Building your new paradigm**
	I choose to be a person of character by being truthful when in relationship with others.
Stage 3.	**Support strategy**
	I choose my new habit of practice/strategy to go above and beyond when communicating by using honesty and truth with others. This will help me to build trust with them.
Stage 4a.	**Create a statement to support your habits and new paradigm**
	My creative and resourceful habits will help me reach my goal:

To go above and beyond in the area of communicating truth with others, I will practice speaking truth in a respectful way. I will listen to the thoughts of others, ask clarifying questions, and be clear about my good intentions.

Stage 4b.   **Highlight key words or phrases in your support strategy**

To go above and beyond in the area of ***communicating truth*** with others, I will practice speaking truth in a ***respectful*** way. I will ***listen*** to the thoughts of others, ***ask*** clarifying questions, and ***be clear*** about my ***good intentions***.

Stage 5.   **List the highlighted key words from your support strategy**

- Communicating truth
- Respectful
- Listen
- Ask
- Be clear
- Good intentions

Stage 6.   **Desired outcome**

The outcome I hope to experience with truthful and respectful communication is a healthy dialogue when communicating with others. I commit to listening well and asking helpful and clarifying questions. I will lead myself with my good intent.

Now It Is Your Turn

Design Your CHARACTER Blueprint

Stage 1.   **Character statement**

We have provided a statement for your focus on building your character.

Integrity builds trust with others.

Stage 2.   **Building your new paradigm**

You will choose a new paradigm focus from one of the four options below.

Your new paradigm focus will become your support statement for building your character.

You may want to think of a problem you need to solve with the above character statement. Solving the problem will require you to have a new paradigm, a new strategy, and a new practice of habits for a better outcome.

Choose **one** of the following mindsets to support the character statement. Your mindset will help you build a new paradigm:

1. Be honest: a person others believe in
2. Be trustworthy: a person who cares about others

3. Be truthful: a person who speaks truth

4. Be reliable: a person who is faithful and responsible

I choose to

_____

_____

Stage 3.   **Support strategy**

This gives you an opportunity to choose the new habits that will support your new paradigm of your character.

You will choose a habit to practice from a list of options that will help you implement your new paradigm in building your character.

From these six choices, choose one habit to practice:

1. Look for ways to go above and beyond in my tasks at work and home.
2. Admit responsibility for failures and mistakes.
3. Be dependable and open to accountability from others.
4. Choose wise decision-making practices.
5. Accept and respond to constructive criticism.
6. Be open to the views and opinions of others.

I choose to

_____

_____

Stage 4a.   **Create a statement to support your habits and new paradigm**

You will need to be creative and resourceful. Think of a new habit or habits that you want to practice every day, which will support your new habit of choice.

Your habit(s) of choice will support your new paradigm and build a strategy to increase in the area of your character.

Write your thoughts below:

_____

_____

_____

Stage 4b.   **Highlight key words or phrases in your support strategy**

Go through your above statement and highlight key words.

Stage 5.   **List the highlighted key words from your support strategy**

Your key words will become memory markers for your practice of strategy.

I will choose to focus on the following words:

_____

_____

_____

_____

Stage 6. **Write your desired outcome**

Keep your desired outcome in mind. You are encouraged to stay focused on your new paradigm, habits, and strategy every day.

_____

_____

_____

You are worth it, and you can do it!
A commitment to being a person of
CHARACTER
with a focus on your strategy and practice …
is worth it.

WEEK TWO

DESIGNING YOUR COMPETENCE BLUEPRINT

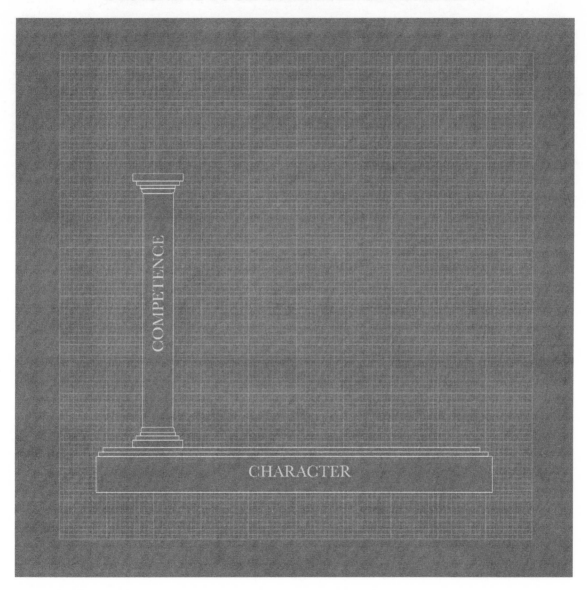

Take your personal and professional temperature on COMPETENCE:
On a scale of 1 to 5 (1 being low and 5 being high), how do you rate the way you lead your life with Competence?

Do you see a difference in how you scored yourself from last month?
To refresh your memory, look at page 21.

Describe any changes you've seen as you've focused on building your competence.

Is transformational change in your competence needed in your life, family, or career?

Explain your thoughts:

Key words for building your COMPETENCE strategy

Dedication
Learning
Communication
Time management
Opportunity

Synopsis of the daily "Competence focus" from every Tuesday in Part 1:

- Your Competence increases when you dedicate yourself to being a lifelong learner. To increase your knowledge, intellect, skills, and talents, you will need to be willing to learn, unlearn, and reshape your current paradigms and ways in which you do things.
- As a Competent person, you will stay focused on transparent communication. Your transparency will bring clarity and understanding for others and you.
- As a person who strives to maintain the highest level of Competence; you will prioritize and manage your time effectively. Period.
- As a Competent person, you <u>act</u> when you see an opportunity. You will increase your level of competence as you respond with a sense of urgency. Your willingness to take immediate action when it is necessary will impact your personal and professional performance in ways that you cannot imagine.

A person of competence understands the reality of their skills and knows how they bring value to their relationships and work with their expertise. They are able to build trust with others through their well-known capabilities, qualifications, and experiences.

COACHING QUESTION

Ask three of your close family members or peers if they find you competent and skilled in the work you do, and why or why not.

Record their responses:

1)

_____

_____

2)

_____

_____

3)

_____

_____

The practice of competence and being willing to learn, unlearn, and reshape your paradigms begins with an individual study of the life and actions of a person you see who has these qualities. Think of someone you know who exemplifies this essential pillar of *Competence* qualities.

What are their key behaviors?

_____

_____

_____

_____

Are there specific qualities within those behaviors you value with regard to their Competence?

_____

_____

_____

_____

When we think of competence, LEADERSHIP comes to mind. Here is why: Competent leadership of self and others creates a cultural mindset of "we can always be and do better together." Leadership leads others with a focus on allowing room for these three key elements:

1) Learning something new
2) Unlearning what is not working
3) Reshaping present learning to achieve future goals and outcomes

No matter what your …

- Intellect and skill sets
- Position or job
- Level of income
- Living and traveling experiences
- Collection of toys in your garage

Leading your own self with a strategy of Competence …matters.

When leading yourself well, your competent leadership reflects the following characteristics:

- You are a role model for transformational change.
- You exhibit core values.
- You lead with both a personal and professional philosophy.
- You are someone whom others want to invest in and retain.
- You have a track record for outstanding performance compared with others.
- You have a broad range of experiences and an ability to learn and adapt quickly to new and unfamiliar situations.
- You demonstrate unparalleled leadership qualities.
- You are competent in using your skills in what you do and how you do it.

Dan's Observations on Competence

Competence is a funny thing. In leading salespeople, I have observed "great at tasks" versus "great at building relationships" when it comes to competence.

A sales person can be consistently competent with getting tasks done, completing projects, reaching their daily sales calls and numbers and yet, lack basic people skills. They have an inability to relate well with others and build strong relationships. This creates consistent relational challenges in and outside the office.

This high level of consistent incompetence in their inability to create relationships with others builds a lack of trust with others, frustration, and possible contempt. If not watched closely, this incompetent person can fake "competence" for a period of time, but the truth will come out as fewer and fewer people desire to work with them and support them.

The sales person who is able to be consistent in their tasks, projects, meeting their sales calls and numbers, along with the ability to build strong relationships, exhibits a high competent behavior and the results are evident and rewarded. People want to work with them and fully support their success.

The reality in coaching salespeople:

- The lack of competence will always be revealed in results.
- Those who are competent and create consistent relationships will have good results.

Results communicate a basic level of truth and reality, which are valuable allies to those in the sales profession, and for all of us. Without truth and reality, a sense of personal denial is created. At some point, denial becomes unsustainable as the unreality created by deceiving oneself comes crashing down.

A Cautionary Tale:

A longtime veteran salesperson loses more than 30 percent of his business over a three-month period. After conducting a postmortem, two main reasons are discovered:

The first problem:

A competitor has assertively gone after two of his largest accounts.

But this is a regular part of business. Having competition in two large accounts can be unsettling and annoying, but should never be unexpected.

So why is this a huge problem?

1) It's a problem because this salesperson carries only 15 accounts in an industry where the average book of business consists of 50-70 accounts.
2) His lack of account volume and diversified business has left him vulnerable, creating a situation in which any attack will automatically elevate the level of threat from "major annoyance" to "potential catastrophe."

It is easy to see that this salesperson has a major problem in the basic structure of his business. To carry less than 25 percent of the industry average account base is a huge deficiency in his business competence. Certainly, he has the ability and competence to find new business. Unfortunately, he has neglected to use this competence in going after new business because he was already making "good money" with his existing account base. He had a paradigm that his "good money" income would last and be sustainable. Further, he used his "I make good money" mindset to justify his lack of competence regarding his book of business.

His second big problem:

He welcomed the attacks.

What? That's crazy, you say. I agree. Why would someone welcome an attack on his business that would threaten his "good money" income stream?

For the same reason things happen all the time in business and life:

The status quo is regarded as good enough – until it isn't.

Here is why his competitor's attack worked:

1) He wasn't calling on the accounts on a consistent basis. This left his customers open and willing to entertain visits from competitors. His lack of consistent calls diminished his customer loyalty.
Lack of personal face time with any client will leave that client open to new opportunities. It's hard to reject a vendor who is consistently calling on your place of business and showing competence in their approach.

2) In both accounts, his costs, on two specific items was way out of line with the market. Unfortunately, these two products made up more than half of his total business in the accounts. He was selling both items at a price nearly twice as high as the industry average. When his decisions for pricing products were exposed by his competitor, he lost all credibility. His defense: "I don't sell these products to many accounts so I wasn't aware of the market price." (Another downfall of the low-account-volume approach, leading to lower levels of competence.)

This salesperson earns multiple hundreds of thousands of dollars per year, and yet, he doesn't know the basic market prices of his most profitable products? This is not incompetence. This is ignorance. It is also something more, it is his ego getting the best of him, and it proved costly.

The denial of truth and reality will lead this salesperson further along a downward spiral, or he can choose to build his competence and consistency and thereby improve his trust and relationships with others.

An Exemplary Tale:

I have also seen the positive side of competence play out in real time: Several years ago, I worked as a sales rep in Houston and I had an oil and gas industry client who used a very large volume of packaging. About six months into my relationship with this customer, I was introduced to the company's Director of Procurement. We'll call her Susan.

Susan needed help creating a standard operating procedure for her vendors to follow as they sent inbound shipments to their facility. We met one morning and spent 20 minutes discussing her company's goals for the new procedures.

Here is how I solved the problem:

1) I promised her that I would proofread my notes and send her a formal document that evening.
2) I followed through on my commitment and sent it as promised. She thanked me, and I never heard from her again. Three months later, I found out that she had resigned. Oh, well.
3) I continued to work with my existing buyer and developed the account into a solid piece of business.

Several months later, I received a voicemail from Susan. She communicated that she had gone to work for another company on the other side of town. She asked if I would be willing to come and observe the packaging process at this new company. This new company became a monster account. Huge rewards were reaped, all from the credibility gained from a single 20-minute display of competence.

> **"Leaders may be aware of the degree to which they actually have the capabilities to do what they say. And if they lack the competence they must dedicate themselves to continuously learning and improving."**
> JAMES M. KOUZES AND BARRY Z. POSNER

Tess Discusses How Clients Use Competence

The following is a sample of four personality based focuses and strategies in building leadership effectiveness through Competence by knowing why you respond the way you do and how to enhance your responses. You may want to highlight the statements that resonate with you:

Extroverted Leadership

If you are an extroverted leader and highly expressive and enthusiastic, you will increase your leadership effectiveness by:

1) Recognizing your propensity to say whatever is on your mind and curbing that propensity when appropriate.
   a. Strategy:
      - Refrain from saying everything that is on your mind.
      - Discipline yourself in how much information you share.
      - Be selective in choosing what you communicate.

2) Identifying when you are being overly enthusiastic.
   a. Strategy:
      - Stop and ask yourself if you are overwhelming others with your enthusiasm.
      - Ask yourself if you are overriding the thoughts and views of others.
      - Seek input from others.

Introverted Leadership

If you are an introverted leader who is private and enjoys solitude, you will increase your leadership effectiveness by:

1) Recognizing when it is important to voice your concerns and share your thoughts and opinions.
   a. Strategy:
      - Speak up to indicate to others that you are interested in the issue and its outcome.
      - Stay open and engaged with others, rather than shutting down and being uninterested.
      - Be willing to express your thoughts and views without a lot of internal time to process and analyze.

2) Identifying when you are being too private and hard to get to know
   a. Strategy:
      - Be willing to initiate and introduce yourself to others.
      - Engage with more than one or two people at social gatherings.

- Know that people are interested in your thoughts and opinions.
- When an issue is important to you, be willing to assert your point of view.

Logical Leadership

If you are a leader who makes your decisions based on using logic, reasoning, and asking questions, you will increase your leadership effectiveness by:

1) Recognizing your propensity to ask too many questions during conflicts.
   a. Strategy:
      - Be clear about communicating your intent.
      - Understand that others may feel different about the issue; it is your responsibility to keep your own emotions in check.

2) Identifying conflict immediately and approaching resolution with a willingness to communicate.
   a. Strategy:
      - Make sure your approach fits the situation.
      - Recognize that healthy conflict can lead to a better outcome and allow goals to be set.
      - Often, the issue is less about the conflict and more about working through and communicating clearly on the issue, then building understanding as to the issue's root cause.

Considerate Leadership

If you are a leader who makes your decisions based on how you feel, what you value, and what you believe is best for the whole, you will increase your leadership effectiveness by:

1) Recognizing when your need for harmony clouds the issue.
   a. Strategy:
      - Understand that constructive criticism is helpful in solving complex issues.
      - Be mindful that others who may not agree with you may want to add their perspectives.

2) Monitoring how much time you spend on building consensus.
   a. Strategy:
      - Know when you need to push others toward action.
      - Be mindful of pushing others toward your own view without the benefit of a healthy dialogue.

You'll notice that each of these leadership-coaching commentaries includes a focus, strategy, and practice to increase leadership effectiveness.

Sample Blueprint for Building Your Leadership Through Your Competence
Before we begin this exercise, read this sample blueprint in its completed form.
You can refer back to this completed sample when building your own blueprint for your Competence.

WEEK 2 – COMPETENCE
Building your blueprint for your Competence

Stage 1. **Competence statement**
Increase my ability to listen, learn, and absorb new information.

Stage 2. **Building your new paradigm**
I choose to reshape my paradigm about my team when working on difficult projects with them.

Stage 3. **Support strategy**
How I convey my thoughts, views, and opinions to others is important to my outcome.

Stage 4a. **Create a statement to support your habits and new paradigm**
My creative and resourceful habits will help me reach my goal.
When I am working with my team on a difficult project, it will be helpful for me to listen to my team members and hear what they are thinking. I will receive and take in new information when my habit of choice is to listen first, then appropriately convey my thoughts, views, and opinions to others. My ability to incorporate new competencies will help me to reshape my paradigm(s) about team members when I begin to struggle with them individually or as a group. My goal for mutual agreement and moving forward will help me to stay focused.

Stage 4b. **Sample highlighting of key words or phrases in your support strategy**
When I am working with my team on a difficult project, it will be helpful for me to *listen* to my team members and *hear* what they are thinking. I will receive and *take in* new information when my habit of choice is to listen first, then appropriately *convey* my thoughts, views, and opinions to others. My ability to incorporate new competencies will help me to *reshape* my paradigm(s) about team members when I begin to struggle with them individually or as a group. My goal for *mutual agreement* and moving forward will help me to stay focused.

Stage 5. **List the highlighted key words from your support strategy**
- Listen
- Hear
- Take in
- Convey
- Reshape
- Mutual agreement

Stage 6. **Desired outcome**
The outcome I hope to experience when working through challenging situations with my team on difficult projects is to listen well to my team members. I want to accurately hear what they

are saying to me. I will choose to be open and respectful as I take in their new information and convey my own thoughts and views. I want my leadership to bring mutual agreement and a positive work environment. I know all good things happen when I have the right paradigm of others and myself.

Now It Is Your Turn

Design Your COMPETENCE Blueprint

Stage 1.   **Competence statement**
We have provided a statement for your focus on building your competence.
Increase my ability to listen, learn, and absorb new information.

Stage 2.   **Building your new paradigm**
You will choose a new paradigm focus from one of the three options below.
Your new paradigm focus will become your support statement for building your competence. You may want to think of a problem you need to solve with the above competence statement. Solving the problem will require you to have a new paradigm, a new strategy, and a new practice of habits for a better outcome.
Choose **one** of the following mindsets to support the competence statement. Your mindset will help you build a new paradigm:
1. Be open: Learn something new.
2. Be teachable: Unlearn what is not supporting your movement forward.
3. Be willing: Reshape your paradigms.

I choose to

Stage 3.   **Support strategy**
This gives you an opportunity to choose your new habits to support your new paradigm of your competence.
You will choose a habit to practice from a list of options that will help you implement your new paradigm in building your competence.
From these six choices, choose one habit to practice:
1. Communicate with my highest level of clarity and honesty.
2. Assess the way I convey my thoughts, views, and opinions with others.
3. Be precise and reasonable when exchanging information.
4. Listen well to others and hear what they are really saying to me.
5. Prioritize and manage my time effectively to achieve my priorities.
6. Join others and act when I see an opportunity (take a leap of faith).

I choose to

_____

_____

Stage 4a.   **Create a statement to support your habits and new paradigm**
You will be creative and resourceful. Think of a new habit or habits that you want to practice every day, which will support your new habit of choice.
Your habit(s) of choice will support your new paradigm and build a strategy to increase your competence.

Write your thoughts below:

_____

_____

_____

Stage 4b.   **Highlight key words or phrases in your support strategy**
Go through your above statement and highlight key words.

Stage 5.   **List the highlighted key words from your support strategy**
Your key words will become memory markers for your practice of strategy.
I will choose to focus on the following words:

_____

_____

_____

_____

Stage 6.   **Write your desired outcome**
Keep your desired outcome in mind. You are encouraged to stay focused on your new paradigm, habits, and strategy every day.

You are worth it, and you can do it!
A commitment to being a person of
COMPETENCE
builds skills, self-awareness,
and a practice of new habits …
it is worth it.

WEEK THREE

DESIGNING YOUR CONSISTENCY BLUEPRINT

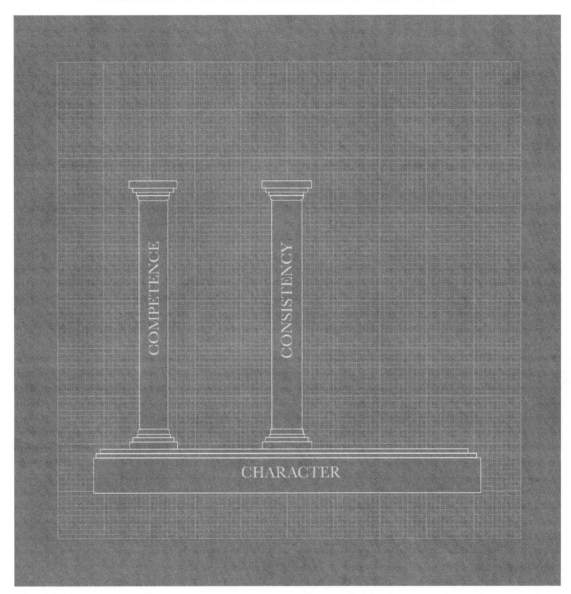

Take your personal and professional temperature on CONSISTENCY:

On a scale of 1 to 5 (1 being low and 5 being high), how do you rate the way you lead your life with Consistency?

Do you see a difference in how you scored yourself from last month?
To refresh your memory look at page 31.

Describe any changes you've seen as you've focused on building your consistency.

_____

_____

Is transformational change in your ability to stay consistent needed in your life, family, or career? Explain your thoughts:

_____

_____

Key words for building your CONSISTENCY strategy

Preparation
Reflection
Intention
Practice

Synopsis of the daily "CONSISTENCY Focus" from every Wednesday in Part 1:

- Consistency requires you to prepare, train, equip, and increase your capacity for strong and predictable leadership behaviors. There will always be known and unknown things that come your way in life and work. Preparing yourself to be resilient within the strengths of your leadership will influence your outcomes.

- An effective strategy will create Consistency. Be honest with yourself and reflect on the way you do things. Are you purposeful in your approach? Do your procedures work? Do you have an effective routine?

- Consistency means you will intentionally follow through on your commitments and keep your promises. Being loyal and dedicated are all quality actions of Consistency.

- Consistency will develop as you continually practice repeatable and reliable behaviors.

A consistent person is known for being reliable. They are able to build trust with others by creating predictable structures, systems, and measurable results. They also have the ability to stabilize situations.

COACHING QUESTION

Ask three of your close family members or peers if they find you competent and skilled in the work you do, and why or why not.

Record their responses:

1)

_____

_____

2)

_____

_____

3)

_____

_____

The practice of Consistency – having predictable behaviors that a person has trained, equipped, and prepared for – begins with an individual study of the life and actions of a person you see who has these qualities. Think of someone you know who exemplifies this essential pillar of *Consistency* qualities.

What are their key behaviors?

_____

_____

_____

What specific qualities in those behaviors stand out to you with regard to their Consistency?

_____

_____

_____

_____

Practical Application From Dan

At my company, we utilize a sales process that is rooted in the quality of consistent behaviors. This is by design. As a sales organization, our biggest challenge is the mountain of negative sales experiences that our prospective buyer clients have experienced. Their own firsthand knowledge has created this paradigm: "Salespeople do not deserve my time on any given day."

This typical response has developed a hardened shell of cynicism toward salespeople. This is the first of many obstacles my salespeople must overcome if they are going to find success in our business. The only way they overcome this obstacle is through their own competence and their personal commitment to consistent behaviors that display that competence. Our salespeople who are predictably consistent with their competence build trust with their current and future clients.

Our salespeople follow our consistent sales process by making nearly 200 account visits a month. In the packaging industry it can take five or more face-to-face visits before a buyer will work with us. Most salespeople give up after just two or three calls.

The client rarely realizes that not only did the salesperson's persistence pay off, but the rep's consistency over time also won them over.

I have found consistency allows our salespeople to prove their own worth and professionalism with predictability. This consistent approach overcomes cynicism.

Right now, if you are a salesperson who is not achieving your goals, it is likely you have played right into your future buyers' previous bad experiences and cynicism. You can turn your outcomes around by choosing to be consistently predictable and competent. These qualities go hand in hand.

The ability to be consistent benefits all aspects of your client relationship. Being a creature of habit is most useful in establishing and sustaining accounts.

So what is the outcome?

1) Our salespeople develop good and healthy client relationships.
2) They understand what their customers need.
3) They provide outstanding service.
4) They go above and beyond for their clients.
5) Our salespeople often take over ALL the business, because there is no one better.

A real-life example: One of the most rewarding days of my sales career was with an owner of a large mail-order pharmaceutical company. He was a decent customer for me whom I had developed over the previous two years. As we walked through his warehouse, I didn't realize that everything was about to change. He turned to me, waved his hand across the enormous space and asked, "So … what else can I buy from you?"

The entire warehouse was in front of me! And he wanted to give me as much business as possible. I had crossed the threshold from "vendor" to "valuable business partner."

The account tripled in size in the next 12 months as the company began to buy every consumable product they could purchase from me.

My character and competence, combined with my consistently predictable behavior, had achieved a level of trust with this owner – so much so that he was willing to give me all of his business. This was a great reward for staying the course and being consistent.

A Coaching Challenge:
Start watching for consistent behavior (or the lack of it) in yourself and others. Consistency, and the lack of it, is everywhere. You can be a voice for "let's create paradigms, processes, skill sets, systems and relationships that help us stay consistently predictable."

Coaching Observation by Tess:
I observe consistency every day when engaged with my clients. You may be interested to know that your consistency patterns are noticeable to others.

> I find my clients consistent in the way they structure their daily lives. Some thrive on life and work being busy, crazily unpredictable, and constantly in motion.
> Others thrive on life being very methodical with a lot of structure and organization. Their schedules, plans and methods for doing things are well thought out. They thrive with their highly controlled behaviors in both life and work.

Both consistent behaviors have the opportunity to be effective with the right focus and paradigm. Your leadership ability to build your personal self-awareness will help you to self-manage your approach to what your employees, organization and relationships need.

A mindful and thoughtful leader will watch for:

> A leadership approach that creates daily chaos, resulting in people around them becoming burdened, burnt out, and negative.
> A leadership approach that creates such tight controls and ways of doing things that people around them become frustrated, pessimistic, and even angry.

It is a leadership reality, the more highly emotional intelligent leadership you understand and implement in the context of your relationships, the greater impact you have on those you lead and serve by the way you do things and get things done.

Another area of consistency I observe with my clients:

> They are consistent in the way they communicate with me. Some communicate every detail and like to make sure I understand the importance of those details.
> Others communicate with general thoughts covering a wide range of ideas and opinions. They trust I am able to connect the dots of their communication style.

Both ways of communicating are appropriate and necessary. Good outcomes are reached on behalf of my clients, even though they use different communication styles.

A mindful and thoughtful leader will watch for:

A leadership approach that creates so many details that the ability to remember all of them becomes impossible for others to follow.

A leadership approach that creates so many different ideas and varying opinions that no one knows where they are going or whom to follow establishes an uncertain and insecure culture.

As a highly emotionally intelligent leader, you will understand the impact your communication has on those you lead and serve.

When engaged in a coaching relationship with my clients, I create consistent and focused meetings. Our coaching meetings provide a time to process, learn, and grow as I help them to develop their leadership over a period of time. When they begin to experience a transformational change, their decision-making process and communication changes. They become leaders who are consistent in balancing appropriate care for others and the use of good analysis when reaching goals. And, they create a work culture that others want to be a part of and contribute to because there are consistent expectations for raising the bar and meeting the expectations. Consistency creates a win-win for all.

A Great Example of Consistency

Coach John Wooden, the great UCLA basketball coach who produced 12 NCAA championships teams (7 of them in a row!) during the 1960s and 1970s, exemplifies the power of consistency.

At the beginning of every new basketball team year, the team learns how to tie their shoes:

"First, put your socks, slowly with care, over your toes, says the coach. The seniors diligently follow instructions. Now, move your socks up here … and here … smooth out all the wrinkles … nice and tight … take your time, the coach intones like some sort of far-out Zen master teaching how to make tea as a path to higher enlightenment. Then lace your shoes from the bottom, carefully, slowly, getting each pass nice and tight … snug! snug! snug! snug!"

"After the lesson, a new team player would ask one of the All-American seniors what that was all about, and he would say, 'Get a blister in a big game, you're gonna suffer. Shoes come untied in a close game … **well, that just never happens here**.'" (a condensed quote and emphasis added)

It "never happened there" because they *consistently* tied their shoes with *competence*. Amazing how this works, isn't it?

Sample Blueprint for Building Your Leadership Through Your Consistency
    Before we begin this exercise, read this sample blueprint in its completed form.
    You can refer back to this completed sample when building your blueprint for your Consistency.

WEEK 3 – CONSISTENCY

Stage 1.   **Consistency statement**
                    Be willing to consistently practice and be prepared.

Stage 2.   **Building your new paradigm**
                    I choose to train myself to be a consistent person.

Stage 3.   **Support strategy:**
                    Create consistent and positive experiences with and for others.

Stage 4a.   **My creative and resourceful habits will help me reach my goal**
                    My habit of choice is to be a person who creates consistent and positive experiences with and for others. It will require me to practice a mindset of being positive. I will commit to using a proactive communication style that is encouraging, helpful, and optimistic. Even my body language needs to be positive, so I will develop actions such as looking people in the eyes when I am talking with them. My willingness to practice and prepare will add value to my personal and work relationships.

Stage 4b.   **Highlight key words or phrases in your support strategy**
                    My habit of choice is to be a person who creates ***consistent*** and ***positive*** experiences with and for others. It will require me to ***practice*** a mindset of being positive. I will ***commit*** to using a proactive communication style that is ***encouraging, helpful, and optimistic***. Even my ***body language*** needs to be positive, so I will develop actions such as looking people in the eyes when I am talking with them. My willingness to practice and prepare will ***add value*** to my personal and work relationships.

Stage 5.   **List highlighted key words from your support strategy**
- Consistent
- Positive
- Practice
- Commit
- Encouraging
- Helpful
- Optimistic
- Body language
- Add value

Stage 6.   **Desired outcome**

The outcome I hope to experience when communicating with others is to add consistent value to our dialogue. I will keep in mind the perceptions of others and use positive body language. I will consistently look people in the eye when I am talking. I will use encouraging, helpful, and optimistic words and commit myself to a positive interaction. Most importantly, I will practice an internal optimism – having thoughts that desire the best outcomes for others and myself.

Now It Is Your Turn

Design Your CONSISTENCY Blueprint

Stage 1.   **Consistency statement**
We have provided a statement for your focus on building your consistency.
A willingness to consistently practice and be prepared.

Stage 2.   **Building your new paradigm**
You will choose a new paradigm focus from one of the three options below.
Your new paradigm focus will become your support statement for building your consistency. You may want to think of a problem you need to solve with the above consistency statement. Solving the problem will require you to have a new paradigm, a new strategy, and a new practice of habits for a better outcome.
Choose one of the following mindsets to support your consistency statement. Your mindset will help you build a new paradigm:

1. Be able: Train yourself to be the person you want to be.
2. Be responsible: Equip yourself to do what you need to do.
3. Be willing: Prepare for what you want.

I choose to

_____

Stage 3.   **Support strategy**
This gives you an opportunity to choose the new habits that will support your new paradigm of your consistency.
You will choose a habit to practice from a list of options that will help you implement the new paradigm that will increase your consistency.
From these five choices, choose one habit to practice:

1) Create predictable routines and habits that will build trust with others.
2) Assess current information and research what new information you need.

3) Keep your promises to others and be loyal to them.

4) Rehearse written and verbal communication to have a positive outcome.

5) Create positive experiences with others.

I choose to

_____

_____

Stage 4a.   **Create a statement to support your habit and new paradigm**

You will be creative and resourceful. Think of a new habit or habits that you want to practice every day, which will support your new habit of choice.

Your habit(s) of choice will support your new paradigm and build a strategy to increase your consistency.

Write your thoughts below:

_____

_____

_____

Stage 4b.   **Highlight key words or phrases in your support strategy**

Go through your above statement and highlight key words.

Stage 5.   **List the highlighted key words from your support strategy**

Your key words will become memory markers for your practice of strategy.

I will choose to focus on the following words:

_____

_____

_____

_____

Stage 6.   **Write your desired outcome**

Keep your desired outcome in mind. You are encouraged to stay focused on your new paradigm, habits, and strategy every day.

_____

_____

_____

You are worth it, and you can do it!
A person of
CONSISTENCY
builds trust with others
with a practice of a good and healthy mindset ...
it is worth it.

WEEK FOUR

DESIGNING YOUR CREATIVITY BLUEPRINT

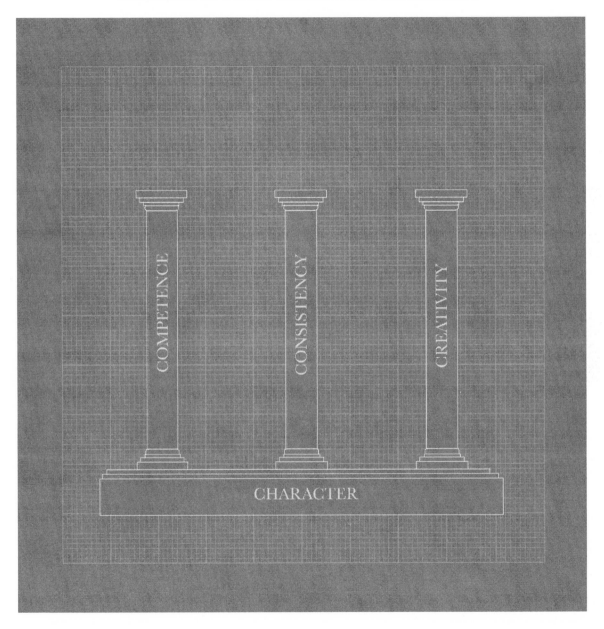

Take your personal and professional temperature on CREATIVITY:
On a scale of 1 to 5 (1 being low and 5 being high), how do you rate the way you lead your life with Creativity?

_____

Do you see a difference in how you scored yourself from last month?
To refresh your memory, look at page 41.

_____

Describe any changes you've seen as you've focused on building your creativity.

_____
_____

Is transformational change in the way you are creative in building strong relationships needed in your life, family, or career?

Explain your thoughts:

_____
_____

Key words for building your CREATIVITY strategy

Change
Curiosity
Overcoming obstacles
Vision

Synopsis of the daily "CREATIVITY Focus" from every Thursday in Part 1:

- Creativity begins when you embrace good and healthy change. You will transform your life when you personally develop a helpful and favorable attitude.
- Building Creative habits, requires curiosity. Being inquisitive and interested in others and having an inquiring mind will lead you to new opportunities and relationships.
- Overcoming obstacles may not seem very creative, yet all problems are solved with varying levels of Creativity.
- Creative people are visionaries. Get out of your box, look around you, and focus on possibilities for you and your future. You get one life, and we encourage you to live it.

An influential person has the ability to create strong relationships and build trust with others. They are able to think of new ideas and process input with others. Their solutions produce excellent outcomes for the good of themselves and others.

COACHING QUESTION

Ask three of your close family members or peers if they find you creative and skilled in the work you do, and why or why not.

Record their responses:

1)

_____

_____

2)

_____

_____

3)

_____

_____

The practice of creativity and the willingness to try new things begin with an individual study of the life and actions of a person you see who has these qualities. Think of someone you know who exemplifies this essential pillar of *Creativity* qualities.

What are their key behaviors?

_____

_____

_____

What stands out to you with regard to their creativity and willingness to try new things?

_____

_____

_____

Coaching Story by Tess

I was facilitating meetings with a board of directors for a nonprofit organization in Los Angeles. They were searching for a new executive director and wanted an outside consultant to guide them through the process. Each board member was well established in the community and successful in his or her respective area of professional expertise. They were highly motivated to choose a new leader.

Their hopes and vision for the new leader were twofold:

1) They wanted the leader to continue to build trust within the community and within the team.
2) They wanted the leader to be prepared to execute goals that would further uphold the vision and mission of the organization.

Three finalists had been chosen for the position. Before the interview process began, I led the members of the board through an exercise and asked them to think about their mutual purpose for the interview process. Even though the board members had a document stating their hopes and vision for a new leader, it was important for each board member to clearly identify the questions they would ask each candidate in order to reach the desired goal. This would give them the ability to hear a candidate's answers and identify where their answers aligned with the hopes and vision of the organization, as well as the roles and responsibilities of a new executive director.

Identifying the questions before meeting with the finalists gave them the opportunity to be united in their purpose and process. If their purposes differed, the main criteria for selecting their new executive director could get lost. I faced the challenge of uniting their questions and aligning their focuses for wanting a new director before they began interviewing the candidates.

A few of their thoughts on mutual purpose were:

1) The candidate should be able to deal with conflict and challenges.
2) The candidate should be able to lead and motivate others.
3) The candidate should have a future vision for the employees and community.

All of their thoughts on mutual purpose were important for the new executive director, but the true mutual purpose was about the quality of leadership needed for the organization to continue to build relationships and trust within the community – the true vision.

The present leader was excellent and had stabilized the organization financially, which was not a small feat during a struggling economy. He had led well and established effective programs for the community. The reality of the present leader leaving the organization was for him to use his strengths and skills for a new opportunity. Yes, it was a loss for the nonprofit and community. It also was an opportunity for the organization to hire a new and competent individual with a new vision.

To build strong relationships with the new executive director and within the community, they would need to transform a team of people to reach new future opportunities and do extraordinary things. The approach would need to be creative and unique to the new executive director and to the team.

Below are areas of focus the executive board used to develop its questions:

- The new executive director would need to express their vision for leadership.
  Question: If you are chosen for the executive director position,
  "What vision do you have for your leadership in leading your team?"

- The new leader would need to be creative in their approach to building new relationships within the organization and outside in the community.
  Question: If you are chosen for the executive director position,
  "How will you build new relationships within the organization and outside in our community?"

- The new leader would need to build upon their strengths, being honest in areas they could improve or increase in their leadership capacity.
  Question: If you are chosen for the executive director position,
  "What are your strengths in leading yourself and others? What is one area where you need to improve or increase in your leadership capacity?"

- The new leader would need to be willing to address issues of conflict.
  Question: If you are chosen for the executive director position,
  "Lead us through how you would handle an issue of conflict with a team member and with a person within the community. How would you follow up in your communication with a person with whom you have had an issue of conflict?"

- The new leader would need to be able to create and develop new programs for the community.
  Question: If you are chosen for the executive director position,
  "How would you go about discerning what new programs the community needs and then go about communicating the new programs to the community?"

- The new leader would need to express their passion for the community, team, and organization. They would need to lead with a creative focus on relationships inside and outside the organization.
  Question: If you are chosen for the executive director position,
  "How will you build relationships within the community? How will you build relationships within the team? And, how will you build relationships within the organization?"

The Strategy for Building Creativity

I tell this interview story because as a leader you should be creative in how you build relationships. When you lead yourself well during the interview process, it is one of the best opportunities to communicate ways in which you create healthy, meaningful and strong relationships. When you communicate effectively with others, you are communicating your personal leadership focus and how you seek to influence your relationships with others. The question a leader often asks themselves on the other side of the interview is this: "Did I answer everything in a way that represented myself in the best of way?" The response is going to be, "I hope so" or "I know I did. I nailed the interview!"

When was the last time you have gone through the interview process? What were the circumstances in finding new employment? Were you seeking a change in career to continue to grow and develop as a leader? Were you let go of a job due to challenges within your workplace? Think about a time when you went through the process of preparing for an interview. Do you have an interview in mind?

Do you remember a potential employer wanting to know how you would work well with others? If so, the employer wanted to assess your ability to cooperate with a board, team, and other employees within the organization.

Many of you have experienced an interview process with several interviewers asking you focused and intentional questions. They wanted to understand logically how you would delegate and accomplish tasks, projects, and goals. They wanted to be convinced that you would bring your intellect, skill sets, and inspiration to solving problems, forging new paths, and creating further financial growth for the organization. They wanted to determine if you were the right person for the job, at the right time, and for the right reasons – They wanted to make sure you were a good fit for the organization. And, the same needs to be true for you. Decide if you are in agreement with the mission and vision of the organization you are seeking employment. Determine if you are the right person for the job and that you are a good fit with the organization you are seeking employment. Being the right fit for a good organization will bring more satisfaction, quality productivity and benefits.

Here are a few questions to think about how you would answer, when you are doing your best to communicate creatively in building strong relationships with others:

- What skills sets do you have that allow you to solve problems with others?
- What communication style will help you to seek and find solutions, plans, or strategies for dealing with complex issues with others?
- What creative ways do you use to gather information and show interest in others?
- Why should others be confident in your leadership?

The Positive Outcome:

In my example, it was ultimately a challenge for the board to consider and decide who the best candidate for the job would be. Initially, no candidate met all of the criteria stated in the mutual purpose. Of course, individual board members preferred one candidate to the other, and for a time, the vote was split between two candidates. As the board assessed what was most critical in the leadership position, they decided on this: The new director needed to have the leadership capacity to express their vision for their leadership and team along with the ability to handle conflict with maturity, confidence, and creativity. It would be important for the new executive director to stay focused on the relationships of the team and the community and yet, the board knew that change would require the ability to manage conflict with others. Once they decided on this direction, the vote was no longer split. When the board reached agreement, they were able to move forward and hire the new executive director. Every board member was satisfied and confident with his or her decision. More importantly, every board member communicated their full support during the transition, as the current executive director moved towards his exit plan and the new executive director created her plan to enter into her new role and responsibilities.

> "Success is peace of mind,
> which is a direct result of self-satisfaction
> in knowing you did your best
> to become the best that you are capable of becoming."
> JOHN WOODEN

Sample Blueprint for Building Your Leadership Through Your Creativity
Before we begin with this exercise, read this sample blueprint in its completed form.
You can refer back to this completed sample when building your own blueprint for your Creativity.

THE PILLAR OF CREATIVITY
WEEK 4 – CREATIVITY
Building your blueprint for your CREATIVITY

Stage 1.   **Creativity statement**
Make a difference and embrace my creativity.

Stage 2.   **Building your new paradigm**
I choose to become more self-aware (know who I am), in order to grow and develop my creativity with others.

Stage 3.   **Support strategy**
I will choose my new habit of practice / strategy to be interested in others and ask thoughtful questions when communicating with them.

Stage 4a.   **Create a statement to support your habits and new paradigm**
My creative and resourceful habits will help me reach my goal. My habit of choice is to be interested in others. My creativity will allow me to ask thoughtful questions of others and be curious about who they are and what they do in their life and work. My new knowledge of others will allow me to build my own self-awareness and be creative as I participate in life and experience new things with them. My creativity will make a difference in my life and the lives of others.

Stage 4b.   **Highlight key words or phrases in your support strategy**
My habit of choice is to be *interested* in others. My creativity will allow me to *ask* thoughtful questions of others and be curious about who they are and what they do in their life and work. My new *knowledge* of others will allow me to *build* my own self-awareness and be *creative* as I participate in life and *experience* new things with them. My creativity will make a difference in my life and the lives of others.

Stage 5.   **Listing the highlighted key words from your support strategy**
- Interested
- Ask
- Knowledge
- Build
- Creative
- Experience

Stage 6.   **Desired outcome**

The outcome I hope to experience when I embrace my own creativity is to make a difference in the lives of others. My new knowledge and self-awareness will bring a mutual benefit when building new relationships. Being interested in others, asking thoughtful questions, and understanding "it is okay to be different" is liberating and creates an enthusiasm within me to further embrace a creative and self-aware life with others. Living with creativity is an opportunity for me.

❖ ❖ ❖

Now It Is Your Turn

Design Your CREATIVITY Blueprint

Stage 1.   **Creativity statement**

We have provided a statement for your focus on building your creativity.
Make a difference and embrace my creativity.

Stage 2.   **Building your new paradigm**

You will choose a new paradigm focus from one of the three options below.

Your new paradigm focus will become your support statement for building your creativity.

You may want to think of a problem you need to solve with the above creativity statement. Solving the problem will require you to have a new paradigm, a new strategy, and new habits for a better outcome.

Choose **one** of the following mindsets to support the creativity statement. Your mindset will help you to build a new paradigm:

1. Be mindful: Keep an open mind when adopting something new.
2. Be positive: Have a favorable attitude when transitioning to trying something new.
3. Be self-aware: Exhibit a high level of self-awareness to personally grow and develop in a new way.

I choose to

Stage 3.   **Support strategy**
This gives you an opportunity to choose your new habits to support your new paradigm of your creativity.
You will choose a habit to practice from a list of options that will help you implement your new paradigm in building your creativity.
From these five choices, choose one habit to practice:
1) Stay curious and eager to discover new things.
2) Be interested in others by asking thoughtful questions.
3) Be a good problem solver.
4) Address difficult situations and difficult people.
5) Give myself the permission to focus on future possibilities.

I choose to

_____

_____

Stage 4a.   **Create a statement to support your habits and new paradigm**
You will be creative and resourceful. Think of a new habit or habits that you want to practice every day, which will support your new habit of choice.
Your habit(s) of choice will support your new paradigm and build a strategy to increase your creativity. Write your thoughts below:

_____

_____

_____

Stage 4b.   **Highlight key words or phrases in your support strategy**
Go through your above statement and highlight key words.

Stage 5.   **List the highlighted key words from your support strategy**
Your key words will become memory markers for your practice of strategy.
I will choose to focus on the following words:

_____

_____

_____

_____

Stage 6.   **Write your desired outcome**
Keep your desired outcome in mind. You are encouraged to stay focused on your new paradigm, habits, and strategy every day.

_____

_____

_____

You are worth it, and you can do it!
A commitment to being a person of
CREATIVITY
in learning about others
and building new relationships ...
is worth it.

Well done!

You have completed your leadership blueprints with strategies for 4 of the 5 C's:

Record your *desired outcomes* from each Stage 6 for:

- **Character**

  _____
  _____
  _____

- **Competence**

  _____
  _____
  _____

- **Consistency**

  _____
  _____
  _____

- **Creativity**

  _____
  _____
  _____

You are ready to move on to Part 3. The marginal gains you have made by leading yourself well through your reading, answering questions, creating strategies, and reflection are your gains from here on.

Excellent!

We are happy for you and your progress.

"Whatever it is you are pursuing, whatever it is you are seeking, whatever it is you are creating, be careful not to quit too soon. As my friend Pastor Rob Bell warns: 'Don't rush through the experiences and circumstances that have the most capacity to transform you.' "
ELIZABETH GILBERT / ROB BELL

What is next?
Continue to move forward. Read Part 3, in which we will cover how all of the 4 C's work together while supporting your development of greater Confidence, the 5th C, within you and for your LEADERSHIP.

PART 3

TRACKING YOUR LEADERSHIP PROGRESS

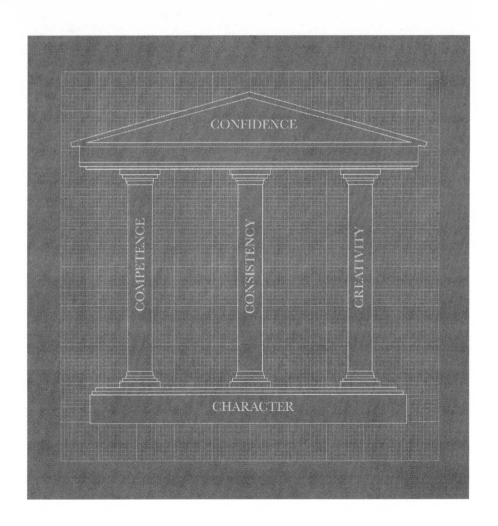

<u>Take your personal and professional temperature on Confidence:</u>

On a scale of 1 to 5, (1 being low and 5 being high), how do you rate the way you lead your life with Confidence:

Do you see a difference in how you scored yourself from two months ago?

To refresh your memory look at page 48.

Describe any changes you've seen as you've focused on building your confidence.

Is transformational change needed in your life, family, and career?
Explain your thoughts:

"Confidence is the most important single factor in this game, and no matter how great your natural talent, there is only one way to obtain and sustain it: work."
JACK NICKLAUS

HOW TO READ PART 3 OF THIS BOOK

Part 3 of "The Leadership Blueprint" continues to focus on your commitment to your personal and professional development as the leader and architect of your life and work.

Over the last two months, you've learned the importance of leading yourself well in your personal life, your relationships, and your career.

Our goal in Part 3 is for you to recognize a new confidence in who you are as the leader of your own life and story. How you lead with confidence in both your personal and professional life ... matters.

As you worked through the first four weeks in Part 1, you participated in a process of daily readings and writings that captured your thoughts and reflections on what you learned. Our goal was to help you increase your level of focus and self-awareness of who you are and why you think and behave the way you do within the 5 C's of Leadership: Character, Competence, Consistency, Creativity, and Confidence.

As you worked through the second four weeks in Part 2, you participated in a focused process of creating a strategy for each of the first four C's: Character, Competence, Consistency, and Creativity. Your focus on strategy led you to create a practice of mindsets and habits for more productive outcomes, greater personal development, and, ultimately, transformational change.

As you work through the final four weeks in Part 3, we ask you to raise the bar of your commitment to yourself. We ask you to take your learning, growth, and development one step further as you focus on the strengths of your growing confidence. You will begin to measure your results in this area as you develop confident mindsets and behaviors.

At this point, you understand that a focused mindset, steps, strategies, and practices are the keys to developing new paradigms and behaviors for transformational change.

During the next four weeks, we ask you to choose one area of focus from Part 1:

- Week ONE - Self-awareness
  - Focused on you building your self-awareness
- Week TWO - Unlocking your potential
  - Focused on you building your ability to unlock your potential
- Week THREE - Stretching above and beyond minimum expectations
  - Focused on you building your ability to stretch above and beyond minimum expectations
- Week FOUR - Influence
  - Focused on you building your ability to influence your outcomes

You will create a strategy for the area upon which you have chosen to focus and begin to practice that focus for the next four weeks. As you practice your steps and strategy, you will be asked to document your outcomes.

As you lead yourself in practice over the next four weeks, you will be asked to gather information. This data and information will help you to recognize significant and meaningful outcomes of change for yourself and others. It will also support your confidence as a leader as you experience good outcomes, and it will encourage you to keep an intentional mindset. Building confidence takes time, focus, and practice.

**"Experiencing transformational change
in being confident is a lifelong practice."**

Let's consider the story of Los Angeles Clippers owner Steve Ballmer, who had this realization about confidence:

You would think that being worth $22 billion would give a person all of the confidence in the world. Yet, Ballmer admits that buying the Los Angeles Clippers for $2 billion was no small feat. An article by Monica Langley in The Wall Street Journal in August 2014 tells of Ballmer "pacing in front of Starbucks on Wilshire Boulevard" before meeting the team. She described Ballmer's demeanor before he met the team for the first time at a dinner as being both "elated and anxious." "He had never been to an event like this before." In the article, he freely acknowledged that he was quite comfortable around software developers and in boardrooms, but to be in a hotel ballroom with a basketball team he had just purchased was a completely new experience for him, and he wanted to be confident. He knew he needed to "find his voice" before meeting the team and its fans. The fact that he was the largest individual shareholder of Microsoft may have been helpful, and certainly gave him influence, yet in a completely different environment. He still needed a newfound confidence in himself and his leadership. He found his voice – "yelling with enthusiasm" – and communicated a trusting confidence that he loved the Clippers organization. All of his reflection, pacing, concern, and nervousness helped him to create a successful event with the team and fans. Over the years, Ballmer's consciously practiced confidence is what inspired the courage to allow him to be true to himself, build relationships with others, and influence a positive outcome for himself and the team. This is powerful leadership in action.

Even for industry titans like Ballmer, confidence ebbs and flows. Achieving influence and excellence requires a high level of resilience and practice. Confidence is a lifelong journey. It requires a constant commitment to building self-awareness in order to accept new realities and seek potential opportunities. As the realities are incorporated into your life and you begin to appropriately exploit opportunities you discover, you will find your reservoir of confidence expanding.

Let's talk about confidence. Here is how confidence functions within the context of designing and building the blueprint for your confident life.

Confidence is:

- An overarching cover that helps you achieve a healthy, competitive advantage for the outcomes you desire.
- A building of your self-awareness and willingness to adjust certain behaviors in order to move forward.
- An unlocking of your potential, which builds strong and effective communication, which in turn builds lasting relationships.
- An ability to stretch and go above and beyond minimum expectations, which affects your commitment to who you are and how you do things.
- An ability to influence others, which keeps you practicing and reaching for a higher vision than you ever thought possible.

If you have made it this far, we applaud you for your commitment to leading yourself with Character, Competence, Consistency, Creativity, and Confidence.

You are on a great leadership journey.
Enjoy!

THE NEXT FOUR WEEKS
DESIGNING YOUR CONFIDENCE BLUEPRINT

Key words to building your CONFIDENCE strategy

Self-aware
Unlock
Stretch
Influence

Synopsis of the daily "Confidence focus" from every Friday in Part 1:

- Increase your capacity to be self-aware.
- Increase your capacity to unlock your potential.
- Increase your capacity to stretch above and beyond minimum expectations.
- Increase your capacity to influence yourself and others.

A person who possesses confidence personally and professionally builds trust with others. The quality of their communication is high, and they excel when resolving conflicts. They are able to influence others through listening, gathering feedback, and collaborating with others to find solutions for best results. Confidence is fully realized through the development of the first four C's.

COACHING QUESTION:
Ask three family members or peers if they find you confident and capable of building trusting relationships.
    Record their responses:

1)
_____
_____
_____

2)
_____
_____
_____

3)
_____
_____
_____

The practice of confidence and the ability to build trusting relationships with others is a worthy goal. Think of someone you know who exemplifies Confidence and has the ability to build trusting relationships with others. What are their key behaviors?

_____

_____

_____

_____

What specific qualities within those behaviors do you value with regard to their Confidence?

_____

_____

_____

_____

Do you know how they gained confidence?

_____

_____

Tess' First Understanding of Confidence

As a child, I was shy, which contributed to my lack of confidence. One of my first memories of being forced to grow in confidence was at 9 years old, when my mother volunteered me to participate in a community Christmas program. I was to read a portion of the Christmas story from the New Testament Scriptures. I was a good reader, yet I was very aware that reading in front of 100 or so people in a large banquet room was going to be quite different from reading to myself, curled up on the couch or reading at school in front of my classmates.

I was not comfortable being in the spotlight. I enjoyed group activities with my friends. Reading in front of a large group of people was going to be a new experience for me, and I knew my part in the program required me to be alone on the platform. Reading by myself, without my friends or support system to help me if I made a mistake, felt "scary."

I was a "practice and prepare" kind of child and took my new responsibility seriously. As I practiced, I became more and more confident of the words that I would be reading. It is one thing to hear a familiar story. It is another thing to know a familiar story and read the exact words of that story in front of people, no matter how many are in the audience. With my practice, the words and phrasing became familiar. And soon, the story, phrasing, and words became internalized – they became part of my memory and inner consciousness. At the time, I had no idea what my practice was doing to help me. I just knew I did not want to make a mistake and embarrass myself in front of others. And I knew I wanted to do well and please my parents.

I don't remember being particularly nervous or excited about reading. I was too young to view my partici-pation as an "opportunity to grow and develop" as a human being. What I do remember is feeling prepared and confident about reading the story. My mind had shifted from being nervous to feeling prepared and confident. When it was time for me to stand in front of a large group of people and read my part of the Christmas story, I actually did very well. As I received affirmation from my parents and others for doing well, I realized that I had enjoyed the experience, and it wasn't so bad after all. Looking back, this was a pivotal personal experience for me as to how I saw myself. I could be in front of people, read out loud, be okay, enjoy myself and feel good about the outcome.

This particular memory had a good outcome. There are other memories that have exceeded my expectations and others that have not, even though I continued my pattern of being practiced and prepared. What I value about this particular memory is that it was the beginning of my being confident in my competence in front of people. From that point on, I have continued to have opportunities to be in front of many people – at times thousands of people – as a speaker, singer, trainer, and teacher.

Building my Character, Competence, Consistency, Creativity, and Confidence began then. Even though at 9, I did not fully understand my opportunity, I do have my mother to thank for volunteering me! I have a greater understanding of how the experience shaped me at the core of my foundation and how it was transformational in shaping my future life and work opportunities.

Dan's First Understanding of Confidence

My first memory of true self-confidence came when I was in high school as I competed in cross-country and track and field.

As a young boy, my parents enrolled me in a local age-group track team to build my coordination. My coordination grew, and so did my love of competitive running. As my skill and ability grew slowly in age-group sports, over the course of several years, I got faster and faster and stronger. By the time I entered high school, I had made massive improvements and was pretty fast in the longer distances. I felt confident in my training and competitive about my ability and speed.

Fast-forward to my freshman and sophomore years in high school: I showed some promise, but nothing spectacular. The summer before my junior year, things seemed to come together as I experienced new teammates and a higher level of competition.

My individual physical development and consistent training effort, along with my seven teammates' consistent development, made us a much stronger team. Our combined efforts helped us win our first invitational meet of my junior season. We beat 20 other high schools by a large margin. At that time, I was the third-fastest runner.

Winning an invitational that large made my teammates and I feel like we had entered the big leagues. We were energized with confidence about our win. On the bus ride home, I remember the atmosphere was electric. We were so excited as we began to envision what would be possible for our team that year.

A few cross-country meets later, we had our first league meet. Five local high schools were competing. I had run well in three or four races that season, and this was shaping up to be a good one for my team and me.

Something interesting happened while I was warming up for the race.

Every parent wants their child to excel at whatever it is they love to do, and my dad was no different. So for that reason, he decided to try something unorthodox with me – at least it was unorthodox for my family.

He told me he'd give me $100 if I won the race.

So, while my running had been pretty good that year and allowed me to help my teammates win, I had never really thought of myself as capable of being "the fastest."

But as a 16-year-old with $100 on the line, I thought, "What the heck; let me try and win this thing."

I won the race easily. No other runner or teammate was even close to me. I led the race from wire to wire. I never expected that to happen. We're talking about more than 40 varsity athletes who all wanted to win – and I beat them all.

My takeaway was this: I had always been able to be competitive, thanks to my training and development. The difference with this particular race was the motivational push from my dad and my friend Ben Franklin.

Somehow, winning that race gave me a whole new paradigm. I began to think of myself as an "elite" athlete. My training, my rest, and my nutrition took on a whole new level of intensity.

Think about this: What truly changed? My body didn't become magically stronger and my skills and strategies for racing were not greatly enhanced. The only thing that changed was how I saw myself.

In the past, I had always trained with the lead group of runners on the team. From that point on, I made it a point to finish my training runs alone and out in front, coming in far sooner than everyone else. Another weird thing happened: Everyone on my own team "let" me take the lead and disappear. I believe that at least two of the guys could have stayed with me, but something had changed mentally for all of us.

The new reality was, I was "faster" than them. I proved this by also winning the second league race, and then the final league championship race, as well.

I became the Foothill League champion of all the area high schools. Our team went on to become CIF Champions for all of Southern California that year.

We were the best long-distance high school team out of hundreds in Southern California. As I reflect on this experience, it's almost hard to believe … but it started in my mind.

Before that first race day in early October, I would never have dreamed that I could go above and beyond in my running capabilities. All my training from early childhood seemed to kick in when I most needed it. My dad may have offered me that first $100 bill as motivation, but he didn't continue to pay me to win races. Looking back, I realize I've had several instances in my life in which I overcame seemingly impossible odds, simply by believing something could be done.

My recipe for success was this: Consistent practice helped me to progress over a reasonable period of time until I built the confidence to believe my winning was possible.

As you develop your Confidence, Character, Competence, Consistency, and Creativity, please realize that you don't need to make flying leaps of progress. One small step a day, over a period of years, will add up to miles and miles of gain.

If you want to succeed with a goal, you need to make sure to put forth the consistent effort in preparing for achievement. It's impossible to achieve anything without first preparing.

Don't forget to take the first step.

> **"Take the first step in faith.**
> **You don't have to see the whole staircase,**
> **Just take the first step."**
> MARTIN LUTHER KING JR.

Your First Understanding of Confidence
Think about your personal story and your first understanding of confidence.

It is now your turn to think about your confidence story. What age were you when you realized you needed confidence to do something out of your normal experience?

_____

When was the first time you had an experience that built your confidence in yourself – in who you are, your abilities, your competence, and what you are able to do?

_____
_____
_____
_____
_____
_____
_____
_____
_____
_____
_____
_____
_____
_____
_____
_____
_____
_____
_____
_____
_____
_____
_____
_____

Tess Finds Inspiration In Confidence

My work in executive coaching affords me many opportunities to observe leaders who exhibit great confidence. I have worked with doctors who are confident in their expertise and ability to care for their patients and lead them to healing and recovery. They continue to build their confidence as they do further research that leads to greater health, for their patients and in the search for cures for diseases.

I have worked closely with senior executives and board members who are tireless in their efforts to execute effective worldwide strategies to reach sales, employee development, financial, and investment goals. They continue to build their confidence as they raise the bar for themselves and others to create greater returns financially and helping their employees thrive.

I have worked closely with the owners of large and small businesses as well as sole proprietors who understand the value of strong, healthy relationships and the use of effective strategies that help their businesses flourish. They understand the need to influence with higher levels of clear, strategic communication and a production level that creates a good work ethic among their employees. They continue to look for ways to build healthy relationships with others in and outside of their business for increasingly successful outcomes.

Most people I have coached have reached high levels of competence. Yet confidence is an area in which every leader desires to grow because their lives and their work require them to increase in confidence with the challenges they face on a daily basis. Many of them are much like Steve Ballmer, the Los Angeles Clippers owner who already possessed a very high level of competence in his corporate life, yet still needed a specialized confidence to succeed in a new situation facing professional athletes. As you, too, focus on leading your own self well, you will find you need to build greater confidence to achieve a higher vision for your life and to be able to experience all that is required of yourself personally and professionally.

Tess Helps A Client Build Confidence Through Communication

One of my clients is a senior executive who works for a large retailer. She needed to prepare a speech for her senior executive team. Every quarter she is responsible for preparing extensive financial information, as well as presenting her team's goals for the next quarter and forecasting achievement through year-end.

She prepared her presentation and asked me to read it and provide feedback.

My client has a strong character and is extremely competent. She provided good information within the context of her speech, but what her speech lacked was a sense of connection and confidence. Her speech was only facts, figures, and data. She needed to ask herself, "How am I going to connect my information to the audience and help them to remember what they have heard?"

Because she had asked me to provide her feedback, I reworked her speech. I emphasized certain words to express her competence and confidence in her facts and figures. I rearranged paragraphs and highlighted certain words so people would be given the opportunity to remember her content. I used what she had written to tell a financial- and employee (team)-based story. I put together an outline form so she had the tools to talk about how her team was working above and beyond and raising the bar in order to reach the financial goals of their company. By refocusing her statements of information into a story line with highlighted words that added meaning to her facts and figures, I helped her to write a more compelling speech. Her subsequent practice and internalizing of her information gave her the opportunity to be a more confident speaker, engage her audience, and focus on the achievements of her team, rather than simply telling her audience what she knew and demonstrating her intellect and competence with a focus on herself. Her speech became about her team and its goals, which would benefit the company.

She found that her confidence in communicating through story increased the executive team's trust in her leadership. She was well received for communicating in a way that increased her ability to be understood. Her confidence moved her and others toward a common goal and vision by creating an energy and experience that others remembered.

Later, I received a note from her, which minced no words:

"THANK YOU – I *was* confident and it went extremely well!"

THE BLUEPRINT OF MY CLIENT'S CONFIDENCE:

- She learned to use a strategy and approach to increase her skills that made her presentation more effective.
- She increased her effort and number of hours she was willing to put into her study and preparation to increase her readiness.
- She practiced in order to ensure her best performance.
- During her presentation, the small wins of her audience appreciating her expertise and her communication, along with strong information, provided encouragement as she moved forward with her presentation.
- Her true and honest communication created a willingness and desire among her audience to follow her leadership.
- Her confidence became part of a larger influence within her organization that she could not have experienced alone.

Dan's Sales Rep Makes a Shift From 'Terrified' to Superstar

As a sales manager in my company's Los Angeles office, I coached a team of 40 sales representatives.

In mid-2014, as one of my new team members began his sales job with the company, he communicated to me that he had started having self-described "night terrors." I thought, "Wow, no one has ever been open enough to communicate 'night terrors' to me before!"

His comment made me stop and think about starting a new job in my industry. It requires a personal commitment and dedication to absorbing massive amounts of product knowledge. It can be daunting and is challenging for the best salespeople.

Trying to absorb the required level of product knowledge and increase in competence in a short period of time is much like drinking water from the proverbial fire hose.

Combining that feeling of being overwhelmed with the pressure of having to hit a quota, and I could see how this salesperson would panic.

We got off to a rough start. I saw that he was prone to panic, and at first, I doubted his abilities – not a recipe for success. Luckily, he had a focused mindset. Here is what I observed:

- He dove into learning what he needed to know to sell our products.
- He faced his daily fear of failure.
- He chose to put one foot in front of the other and make the cold calls necessary to win business.

He consistently exhibited these three behaviors daily, and he called me at least six times a day. I was okay with every call because intuitively I realized he could do it and the hard work would pay off. The hard work absolutely did pay off! He remained employed, finished the company's rookie program, and became veteran sales rep., and consistently exceeds his quota.

Why did this happen?
This salesperson was committed to a good work ethic and took advantage of a good opportunity to increase his capacity for sales.

- He learned and increased his knowledge about our products.
- He faced his fears – daily.
- He focused and made the cold calls.

How did this happen?
With his commitment and consistent ability to follow our sales process, he generated opportunity after opportunity and became more competent about our products and more confident about what he was trying to sell and who he was trying to sell to.

He implemented a meticulous standard of follow-through for every lead he generated.

- He was committed.
- He was consistent.
- He became more competent and confident.

What happened to this salesperson?
With coaching support and several daily opportunities to discuss his challenges, he began to notice the significant habits and behaviors that were working for him and leading him toward success. He capitalized on his marginal gains and repeated those habits over and over.

- He was willing to be coached.
- He was open to dialogue.
- He was self-aware and recognized the habits and behaviors that worked best for him.
- He repeated the habits and behaviors that brought him success,

This salesperson needed a lot of coaching and support. As a leader and coach, I knew one of two things would happen:

1) He would have a mental breakdown and quit.
2) He would power through and embrace the challenge.

I knew that if he were willing to stretch his capacity to learn and use my coaching support and expertise in our products and customer needs, he would come out a superstar.

Luckily for him and for our company, he chose the path of resilience, which led to increased confidence, and now he's a superstar! As a company, we couldn't be more happy for and proud of him.

We have focused on these rules:

- Everything begins with your paradigm.
- You must commit to your personal and professional growth.
- You must consistently move forward.
- You must continue to embrace new levels of confidence.

For the next four weeks, you will focus on building your Confidence.
Transformational change happens when you focus on new paradigms, strategy, and the practice of good and positive habits.

As you think about your own confidence, it is probable you exhibit one or more of the following (feel free to circle or highlight the statements you agree with about your confidence):

You are the author of your own character.
- Confidence built on a strong character foundation gives you the ability to trust your inner self.

You have attained a sufficient level of competence.
- Confidence built on competence gives you the ability to believe in the strengths of your abilities, knowing that you can rise to the challenge with your expertise and skills. It allows you to be open and gain new knowledge.

You are committed to being consistent, expressing what you need and exhibiting consistent behaviors that lead you to build strong and healthy relationships that are supportive and encouraging.
- Confidence gives you the ability to be consistent in your beliefs, philosophy, and behaviors, regardless of your relationships and situations.

You understand that life needs to be creative, whether you are creating relationships with an individual or group of people or focused on individual artistic expression. Creativity is communicated in all that you say and do.
- The ability to stay creative in relationships with others may require you to see things from a different perspective. Creativity stays open, agile, and adaptive to the present moment, person, and situation.

You know what you believe and value. You have a personal philosophy for living a life that is meaningful to you.
- Confidence grows and transforms when you live your life from a base of a personal philosophy. Confidence gives you the space to grow inwardly and helps you to form and develop new insights, habits, and behaviors throughout your life.

You think for yourself and are able to share your thoughts and opinions with others.
- Confidence gives you clarity and purpose in life and in your work with others.

You appreciate and value recognition, but do not rely on the approval of others to derive self worth.
- Confidence leads you to new opportunities because people know and see your value.

You are able to influence the behaviors and opinions of others.
- Confidence does not let your fear of rejection get in the way.

You are able to lead yourself and others well.
- Confidence puts trust in your best intentions. Confidence is present and fully alive, even when you cannot completely know the outcome of your actions.

You are confident in leading effectively with different people and in different situations.
- Whatever you need, confidence is capable of providing.

Confidence cannot be purchased, loaned, or sold; it is an accumulation of good, healthy, and challenging experiences. Confidence is the cumulative impact of taking the other 4 C's – Character, Competence, Consistency, and Creativity – and applying them to all aspects of your life. The qualities of who you are and how you do things with Confidence impact all of your outcomes.

All of your confident choices matter!
Each of your choices has the potential to build your Confidence.

Why is building a Confident mindset important to you?

_____

_____

_____

_____

Write down the Confident characteristic statements you circled/highlighted above and exhibit today.

_____

_____

_____

_____

_____

_____

_____

_____

A brief review of what CONFIDENCE requires:

- Self-awareness
  It grows out of your acquired skills, life experiences, and suitable paradigms.

- Unlocking your potential
  It expands from your learning, knowledge, and practice or from doing things differently.

- Stretching above and beyond minimum expectations
  Having self-awareness of the results of your actions and knowledge of where you may still need to improve gives you the ability to accomplish new goals.

- Influence
  Having the ability to lead your own self and others toward positive outcomes increases their willingness to follow your lead.

These four aspects of Confidence form a continuous loop that allows you to lead a more productive life and influence the well being of others.

Sample Blueprint for Building Your Leadership Through Your Confidence
Before you begin this exercise, read the following completed sample blueprint form.
You can refer back to this completed sample when building your blueprint for your Confidence.

As you reflect on your own confidence, ask yourself the question, "What area will help me build a higher level of confidence in my life and work?"

- Self-awareness
- Unlocking my potential
- Stretching above and beyond minimum expectations
- Influence

WEEK 1 – CONFIDENCE
Building the blueprint for your confidence.

Stage 1.   **Create a confidence statement**
I choose to commit my new learning and growth to becoming more self-aware.

Stage 2.   **Build your new paradigm**
I choose to increase my self-awareness by building trust with others and being a person of integrity.

Stage 3.   **Create a strategy to support your new paradigm**
I choose my new habit to practice to be listening. I want to *really* listen to what others are saying before I judge what I am hearing.
My ability to listen to others will increase trust with them and build a greater level of communication between us.

Stage 4a.   **Create a statement to support your habits and paradigm**
My creative and resourceful habits will help me reach my goal:
to be a person who listens to others. I will practice *really* listening to others before I judge what I am hearing. I want my ability to listen to others to help me to increase trust with them and create greater communication.

Stage 4b.   **Highlight key words or phrases from your statement**
To be a person who *listens* to others. I will practice *really* listening to others first, ***before I judge*** what I am hearing. I want my ability to listen to others to help me ***increase trust*** with others and create greater ***communication***.

Stage 5.   **List the highlighted key words from my support strategy**
- Listen
- Before I judge
- Increase trust
- Communication

Stage 6.   **Describe your desired outcome**
My desired outcome is to increase my self-awareness by building trust with others through increasing my ability to listen to them. I really want to hear what others are saying to me before I judge what they are saying. I hope to build a greater level of communication with new intention and a commitment to listen.

Now It Is Your Turn

Design Your CONFIDENCE Blueprint
Week 1 – A Covering of Confidence

Stage 1.   **Confidence statement**
Choose one of the following areas and create your Confidence statement:

- Self-awareness
- Unlocking my potential
- Stretching above and beyond minimum expectations
- Influence

Write your confidence statement below:

_____

Stage 2.   **Build your new paradigm**
You have chosen your area of focus and Confidence statement from the options above. Now, choose a new paradigm on which to focus from a list of options below:

- Self-awareness: a focus on skills, life experiences and paradigms.
- Unlocking your potential: a focus on learning, new knowledge and practice.
- Stretching above and beyond minimum expectations: accomplishing new goals.
- Influence: leading yourself and others well towards positive outcomes.

Write your area of focus to gain in Confidence below:

_____

Your new paradigm will become the support statement for building your confidence.

Think of a problem you need to solve with the above Confidence statement and new paradigm. Solving the problem will require you to create a strategy, and new habits with your new paradigm in mind, in order to experience a better outcome.

Choose one of the four support statements that are listed below under the Confidence statement you have chosen to support your new paradigm.

Confidence statements:

1. Self-awareness
    a) Building trust with others: Being a person of integrity
    b) Learning: Unlearning and reshaping your paradigm(s)
    c) Being prepared
    d) Embracing good and healthy change

2. Unlocking your potential
    a) Being incredible and raising the bar for yourself and others
    b) Communicating with your highest level of clarity
    c) Using effective strategies
    d) Staying curious in relationships

3. Stretching above and beyond minimum expectations
    a) Admitting responsibility for failures and mistakes
    b) Prioritizing and managing time
    c) Keeping commitments
    d) Overcoming obstacles

4. Influence
    a) Responding to constructive criticism and feedback
    b) Acting when you see an opportunity
    c) Practicing … practicing … practicing
    d) Being a visionary

I choose to

_____

_____

_____

Stage 3.   **Support strategy**
Building new habits to support your new paradigm of Confidence.
You will create your own habits to practice. Ask yourself, "What habit(s) will help me to support my new paradigm in order to practice my confidence statement?"

I choose to

_____

_____

_____

Stage 4a.   **Create a statement to support your habits and new paradigm**

Making behavioral choices – adding healthy support habits for your new paradigm.

You will need to be creative and resourceful. Think of a new habit(s) to practice every day that will support your new paradigm. Your habit(s) will also build the strategy that will help you to increase in confidence.

Write your thoughts below:

_____
_____
_____

Stage 4b.   **Highlight key words or phrases in your support strategy**

Stage 5.   List the highlighted key words from your support strategy. Your key words will become memory markers for you to practice your strategy.

I will choose to focus on the following words:

_____
_____
_____
_____

Stage 6.   **Write your desired outcome**

Keep your desired outcome in mind. Stay focused on your new paradigm, habits, and strategy every day.

_____
_____
_____
_____

Keep your desired outcome in mind. Review this strategy blueprint every morning for the next week. This will keep your Confidence strategy at the forefront of your mind.

Week 2 – The next three weeks will be focused on measuring your results. You will reflect on which habits are working well for you and which need adjustment.

We have provided the sample strategy for building your confidence for your reference. After the sample strategy, we have provided an example of documenting the habits that work well for you and the necessary adjustments needed to achieve better outcomes.

Stage 1.   **Create a Confidence statement**

I choose to commit my new learning and growth to becoming more self-aware.

Stage 2.   **Build your new paradigm**
I choose to increase self-awareness by building trust with others and being a person of integrity.

Stage 3.   **Create a strategy to support your new paradigm**
I choose my new habit to practice to be listening. I want to *really* listen to what others are saying before I judge what I am hearing.
My ability to listen to others will increase trust with them and build a greater level of communication between us.

Stage 4a.   **Create a statement to support your habits and paradigm**
My creative and resourceful habits will help me reach my goal:
to be a person who listens to others. I will practice *really* listening to others before I judge what I am hearing. I want my ability to listen to others to help me to increase trust with them and create greater communication.

Stage 4b.   **Highlight key words or phrases from your statement**
To be a person who *listens* to others. I will practice *really* listening to others first, **before I judge** what I am hearing. I want my ability to listen to others to help me to **increase trust** with others and create greater **communication**.

Stage 5.   **List the highlighted key words from my support strategy**

- Listens
- Before I judge
- Increase trust
- Communication

Stage 6.   **Describe your desired outcome**
My desired outcome is to increase my self-awareness by building trust with others through increasing my ability to listen to them. I really want to hear what others are saying to me before I judge what they are saying. I hope to build a greater level of communication with new intention and a commitment to listen.

Sample: Documenting Habits

Week 1
You created your strategy for building your Confidence. You created a new paradigm of focus and new habits to support your new paradigm. You added those healthy support habits for your new paradigm, focused on your practice, and wrote about your desired outcome.

Week 2
This week, you will document the habits that worked well for you from your desired outcome statement.

Sample of a desired outcome statement:

My desired outcome is to increase my self-awareness by building trust with others through increasing my ability to listen to them. I *really* want to hear what others are saying to me before I judge what I am hearing. I hope to build a greater level of communication with new intention and commitment to listen.

Habits that worked well for me:

1) I chose to be more self-aware when listening to others and not interrupt when they were talking.
2) I chose to listen and let the other person complete his thoughts before I responded to what he was saying. I waited to make sure he was finished with his thoughts before agreeing or disagreeing with him.
3) I chose to listen with my best intent by identifying key words the other person was saying before I responded. When I responded, I chose to address what he was talking about, rather than taking the conversation in a different direction.

On a scale of 1-5 (1 being low and 5 being high) – I give myself a ___2___.

What habits do you need to adjust and improve for week 3?

1) I need to continue to build my listening skills, especially when I want to assert my views and opinions when responding to others. The person I am in dialogue with may or may not be ready to accept my views and opinions. By listening to what the person is saying, I will be better prepared to address them with statements to which they will listen.
2) I know I prefer to talk more than I listen. I want to increase my capacity to listen to what the other person is saying before I assert my views and opinions in any situation.

Week 3
Habits that worked well for me:

1) I chose to be honest with myself and acknowledge that I need to listen to what others are communicating rather than thinking of what I want to say.
2) I chose to be mindful of whether the other person is ready to hear what I have to say.
3) I chose to ask clarifying questions to make sure I was hearing what the other person was saying.

On a scale of 1-5 (1 being low and 5 being high) – I give myself a ___3___.

What habits need to adjusted and improved for week 4?

1) I need to stay focused on identifying when the person I am communicating with is ready to hear my thoughts, views, and opinions.
2) I need to stay mindful that listening really works well when I am intentional about it.

Week 4
Habits that worked well for me:

1) I am listening at a higher level and hearing what the other person is saying without thinking about what I want to say.
2) I am asking good questions to clarify what the person is communicating to me.
3) I am mindful of how ready the person with whom I am communicating is to hear my thoughts, views, and opinions.

On a scale of 1-5 (1 being low and 5 being high) – I give myself a ____4____.

What are three key habits that are working well for me when listening to others?

1) I listened before thinking of what I wanted to say.
2) I asked clarifying questions.
3) I was mindful of how ready the person with whom I was communicating was to hear my thoughts, views, and opinions.

Now it is Your Turn to Document Your Habits

Week 1
Begin with your Confidence statement

_____
_____
_____

Write your desired outcome statement

_____
_____
_____

Week 2
During this week document the habits from your desired outcome statement that worked well for you:

1) _____
_____
_____

2) _____
_____
_____

3) _____
_____
_____

On a scale of 1-5 (1 being low and 5 being high) – I give myself a _____.

What habits need to be adjusted and improved for week 3?

1) _____
_____
_____

2) _____
_____
_____

Week 3
Habits that worked well for me:

1) _____
_____
_____

2) _____
_____
_____

3) _____
_____
_____

On a scale of 1-5 (1 being low and 5 being high) – I give myself a _____.

What habits need to be adjusted and improved for week 4?

1) _____
_____
_____

2) _____
_____
_____

Week 4
Habits that worked well for me:

1) _____
_____
_____

2) _____
_____
_____

3) _____
_____
_____

On a scale of 1-5 (1 being low and 5 being high) – I give myself a _____.

Over the last three weeks, what are three key habits that worked well for me?

Write your thoughts below:

1) _____
_____

2) _____
_____

3) _____
_____

**You are leading yourself well.
It is worth being committed to your
CONFIDENCE in all ways … always.**

You have completed measuring your results for the last of the 5 C's –
Confidence:

Record your *desired outcome* from Stage 6 for:

- **Confidence**

  _____

  _____

  _____

What key habits stand out to you that created greater Confidence for you?

_____

_____

_____

**We want to congratulate you on doing a
GREAT JOB
and committing to the hard work
that has gotten you to this place of
TRANSFORMATIONAL CHANGE!**

**Leading your Life
with Confidence
is a lifelong learning commitment …
YOU MATTER!**

To lead yourself above and beyond – We have provided the final piece of your Leadership Blueprint … it is just ahead…

PART 4

THE LEADERSHIP BLUEPRINT: REFLECTION

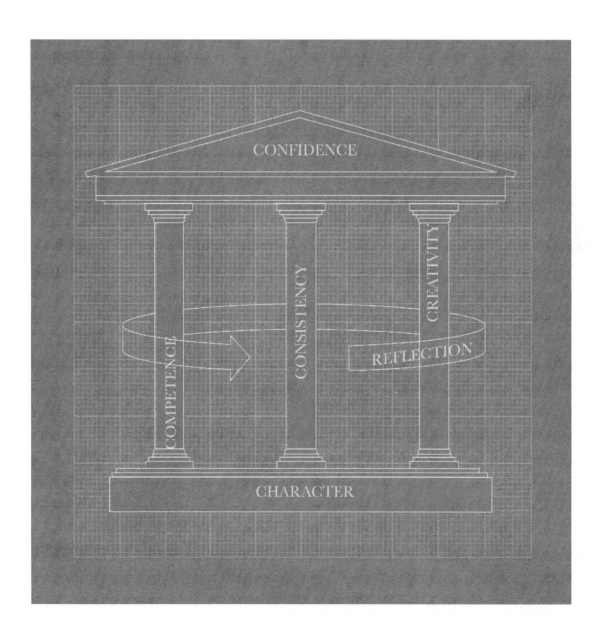

> **"I like the idea of dreaming the big dream and making small steps.**
> **I'd like to think that you reach your hand, just a little bit further than**
> **your reach, not enough so that you'll be frustrated, not enough so that**
> **you'll give up, but just enough so that you'll stretch yourself."**
> MAYA ANGELOU

Reflection: an opportunity of time, as a leader, to give careful thought and consideration as to what is working well, what needs to be adjusted and what needs to change.

You have made a valuable commitment to yourself and your leadership over the last several months. Our hope for you is a transformational change as you have read and worked through the coaching support questions, along with the creation of strategies to lead yourself well by using the Leadership Blueprint.

Your transformational change may have involved the ways in which you see people and things, or the ways in which you communicate with others for clarity and understanding, or the ways in which you work through challenging situations and process difficult decisions.

At this point, we are confident that you have developed the capacity to experience positive results from your hard work in building your leadership – leading yourself, first. Your particular focus and strategy will have created a good foundation for the outcomes you desire. To continue growing, you may wish to revisit Part 2 and Part 3 in the coming weeks and choose a new area of focus on which to continue to expand your leadership capacity with new strategies and measuring your results.

"Reflection" is an interesting word. The word itself may cause feelings of inadequacy if you perceive your reflection to be critical of your efforts and judgmental of your outcomes. More constructively, reflection has the potential to renew your hope and generate further desire, as you want to reproduce your efforts because the experience was so enjoyable and positive.

Reflection gives you the opportunity to give careful consideration to any topic or situation. In Part 4, we ask you to reflect on your strengths as you lead your own self well in the following areas:

1) What strengths underlie who you are personally and professionally?
2) What strengths underlie why you do what you do in life and work?
3) What strengths help you to create a lifetime of meaning?

The above questions may seem broad to you. But upon reflection you will be able to fill in the details of your strengths.

Why reflect on these questions? Your reflection gives you the opportunity to:

1) Recognize your strengths
   - Every day you use certain strengths that work best for you.

2) Utilize your strengths at the highest potential and capacity
   - Every day you have a choice to use your strengths for the best of outcomes.

3) Reproduce your strengths for the good of all
   - Every day you have the opportunity to use your strengths to build connections with others and encourage others.

Personal and Professional Reflection From Dan

My personal and professional strength is my passion. I am committed to the principles I believe in, and the goals I've set out to accomplish. That commitment gives me extraordinary energy. As I work with my co-workers and team, this energy enables me to work long hours, stay positive, and look for the highest and best outcomes that we can affect through our actions.

With my wife, Nichole, I am working to build a relationship and a home that allows every member of our family to feel safety, peace, and joy.

I strive to teach my children moral beliefs and values, along with a lifestyle that creates a vibrant, memorable childhood. My hope is they will choose to do the same for their kids, creating a family legacy. My thought is this: "If I raise my children with intention, I have the potential to reach multiple generations with positive influence. Even if my great-great-grandchildren don't know my name, I can play a role in their lives."

Why am I committed to these things? I've been blessed with some very strong, positive leaders in my life. Their leadership influence, combined with my own natural personality traits, have made for a potent drive and commitment to paying it forward.

I love people! I like to find out new things about them and how to make them feel important. My favorite thing to do during my workday is to be intentionally interested in the new people I meet. I am an extrovert, so this comes as no surprise, but I have observed that my extroversion has amplified in the last 10 years. As I have made it a practice to enjoy people because my sales job requires it, I have found that I've improved at it, and the pleasure I get from this practice has increased. It makes sense … I enjoy doing things I am good at. Why wouldn't I enjoy something even more as my proficiency increases?

How do I do these things? I must go back to positive influences. I have had some great personal mentors, and I've also had some virtual mentors. Listening to Jim Rohn, the business thinker and lecturer, started me down the path of continual personal development. That one concept, personal development, and the results that have stemmed from the pursuit of it, have been the single largest change in my adult philosophy.

That's why writing this book has such an appeal to me. This is a book written to help me advance the development of five very important facets of my life: Character, Competence, Consistency, Creativity and Confidence - the 5 C's, which form the Leadership Blueprint for my life and work.

Personal and Professional Reflection from Tess

As I reflect on my personal and professional leadership strengths, three areas stand out to me –

1) Relationally, I have the ability and privilege to support and participate physically with my family, friends, and clients as we celebrate life, hard work, and love.
2) Resourcefully, I am able to be a source of positive emotional energy and encouragement. I am a sounding board and resource regarding difficult personal issues, as well as important and complex business decisions.

3) Realistically, I help those who entrust their leadership journey to me. My heartfelt and intentional desire is to guide everyone I know to the understanding that they are first the leaders of themselves, and they have choice every single day to lead their lives with meaning and purpose.

Relationships are important to me. As I intentionally bring my best self to my personal and professional relationships, I trust my family, friends, and clients feel heard, understood, cared for, inspired and yes, celebrated!

In turn, my relationships help me to grow and to cultivate further learning and understanding of others. My capacity broadens with deeper and thoughtful communication, which creates new, memorable and long-lasting experiences for all.

As I reflect on my professional leadership strengths and my desire to pay it forward, I know I have the mindset of wanting the best for my clients. I often say, "I always want the best for you." This truth is my starting place of how I think about my clients. My paradigm about who they are is extremely powerful. It impacts every single email, text, phone call, and dialogue. As I am clear regarding my own thought process, my approach, the tone of my voice, the words I choose, and my actions, they all become a part of bringing the highest quality of my leadership to my client relationships. This gives my clients the ability to be honest with their own thoughts and reflections, to discuss complex business issues, dialogue about employee strengths and challenges, and it gives them the opportunity to envision new opportunities for their professional and personal futures.

The opportunity to hear the stories of my family, friends, and clients is deeply meaningful. It is within the context of one's story that lives are built and legacies are achieved. Leaving a legacy of love, building strong relationships, wanting what is best for my clients, and creating meaning in life and work is an intentional focus for me. It is the foundation of my decision-making and how I live my life every day. It gives me happiness to create meaning, and it gives me joy to experience life with others.

Life, Work and Love are to be celebrated. Outside of running my own business with TESS COX & ASSOCIATES, as a coach, consultant, trainer and author, I also have the honor of officiating weddings for family and dear friends. Weddings are stressful on many levels, and it is easy to lose the meaning when there are so many details to accomplish before the "Big Day." Eight years ago, I had the privilege and joy to officiate my son Justin and his bride-to-be, Elaine's wedding. When they, as bride and groom joined hands and faced one another before me and their many family members and friends as witnesses, the only things that mattered were their love and their relationship. Creating meaning for their ceremony of vows and commitment to one another is a priceless memory. In the new 2017 year, I will again have the joy in joining my daughter, Chelsea and her groom-to-be, Vaughn in marriage. The only thing that will matter on their wedding day is their love and their relationship. It will be a joy filled day with family and friends and a great celebration to witness their vows and commitment to one another. This too, is a leadership legacy that I intentionally live for in love and life.

On the other side of celebration is sorrow. Leading others and myself through the sadness of loss is another important aspect to my leadership journey. It is more difficult to lead when there is pain and suffering and yet, life requires us to hold the tension between our joy and our sorrow. The privilege to celebrate lives that have lived and are now no longer physically present brings a comfort and peace to stay focused on what really matters in life and love.

From a business perspective the use of "life and love" may feel too "touchy-feely" for some, and yet the meaning holds true. I take profound pleasure seeing my family, friends and clients thrive, whether they own their own businesses or work for others; and regardless of the complexity and challenges, it is an honor to be a part of their lives. Being an expression of care, being in a relationship, wanting what is best for them, and creating meaning within the context of their roles and responsibilities is what I am intentionally living for. The legacy is the same, yet the words and approach are adapted to the individual and situation.

At the end of the day, my life's joy and satisfaction comes from living, working with, and guiding others to lead themselves in the best of ways towards their desired outcomes. This focus and mindset begins when I make my bed in the morning and stays with me until I lay my head on my pillow at night.

Ultimately, my focus is to lead myself well in all ways and in all things with the 5 C's: Character, Competence, Consistency, Creativity and Confidence – My Leadership Blueprint.

Your Personal and Professional Reflections

Please feel free to refer back to our personal and professional reflections for guidance. What is important? We ask you to give yourself permission to write about you and your 5 C's: Character, Competence, Consistency, Creativity and Confidence.

1) What strengths underlie who you are personally and professionally?

_____

_____

_____

_____

_____

_____

_____

_____

2) What strengths underlie why you do what you do in life and work?

_____

_____

_____

_____

_____

_____

_____

_____

3) What strengths help you to create a lifetime of meaning?

_____

_____

_____

_____

_____

_____

_____

_____

FINAL EXERCISE
COMPLETING YOUR LEADERSHIP BLUEPRINT
Creating a Personal / Professional Philosophy Statement

As you gather all of your learning over the last 90 days, consider this: What personal or professional philosophy statement will help you to be mindful of who you are and why you do what you do in life, relationships and career?

There is no right or wrong way of creating a Personal / Professional Philosophy Statement. The statement is meaningful to you, one that you want to remember and use as a guideline as you continue to create your life.

Write a philosophy statement about your Character:

_____

_____

Write a philosophy statement about your Competence:

_____

_____

Write a philosophy statement about your Consistency:

_____

_____

Write a philosophy statement about your Creativity:

_____

_____

Write a philosophy statement about your Confidence:

_____

_____

Combine all five statements to create your **LEADERSHIP BLUEPRINT**.

_____

_____

_____

_____

_____

_____

_____

WE ARE PROUD OF YOU,
VERY HAPPY FOR YOU,
AND ALWAYS WANT THE BEST FOR YOU!

TESS AND DAN

❖ ❖ ❖

ACKNOWLEDGMENTS

It is with the deepest of gratitude to those who have supported and encouraged us on this journey of writing, "The Leadership Blueprint – Becoming the Architect of Your Life and Work". The collective efforts of many friends and advisors have brought this book into existence. We are forever grateful for their time, expertise, and participation. Our joint efforts raised the bar on all levels for which, we are thankful. Every contribution moved the book process forward.

To Maryanne Dell, our editor, we thank you for your input, great questions and keeping us consistent and clear in our message. You were generous and kind with us and we came to value the "accept edits" tool. Your tireless work while working for others, and the many causes that are also near and dear to you is deeply appreciated. In some way, we became one of your "causes" to get this project right.

To Jeff Geortzen, our graphic designer, we value every bit of your talent and expertise. We know our desire to keep the graphics basic and uncomplicated produced graphics that are well below your skill set. You used amazing restraint and respect to give us the product we asked for. We are forever grateful for your contributions.

Tess' Acknowledgements

Having a writing partner committed to this project, along with being friends for so many years is one of my greatest blessings in life. Dan, your willingness to engage in writing this book when you were also raising a family, working, training sales people, and moving to a new state, has my greatest respect. Thank you for all of your contributions and insights, and for the steadfast desire to see this project through to completion.

We've learned together through this process and have led ourselves with the words we have written – The 5 C's of Leadership. We've embraced honesty, transparency, collaboration and even points of conflict and have made the adventure "fun" and rewarding for both of us. I am blessed to count you, Nichole, and your three children as part of my extended family.

The devoted love and support of my husband Dean and thirty-six years of marriage is a testimony to being my true companion for life. Your leadership, dedication to our family and to me has my profoundest respect and my deepest love. Thank you for entering into the editing phase of the book and contributing your thoughts and ideas. Your input increased the quality and made our writing that much better.

My children are a blessing from God. They are also my biggest fans and cheerleaders! Justin, Elaine, Chelsea and Vaughn…you are my very heart and soul of love. Thank you for your encouragement, love and support. And, thank you for giving freely of your expertise in advertising, marketing, networking and true hospitality. You are ALL amazing and leading your lives well – I am a very proud mom!

How do you thank long lasting friends, generous mentors (both physically and in written form), skilled professors, smart and humble business associates, and exceptional clients who have contributed an abundance of blessings? "Thank you" seems so simplistic, and yet, heartfelt gratitude is ever present. I have not walked the journey of my life, nor learned to lead my life alone. Each one of you (you know who you are) has brought joy, happiness, leadership and fulfillment to my life on so many levels and in so many ways. I am always and forever grateful for learning from you.

When my parents decided to adopt me as their child, little did we know how our story would unfold as a family. The journey of love is ever present now and forever. I am deeply thankful they chose me to be their daughter and I have the blessing of calling them my, mom and dad. Their decision to adopt was the beginning of my leadership story.

Thank you, God. For in You and through You all blessings of good, healthy, respectful and loving leadership flow…

Dan's Acknowledgements

If it weren't for the tireless efforts of my co-author Tess, this book would never have been written. She has been the engine of this project from the start. For nearly 3 years, Tess kept me on track, and kept this endeavor going. She did countless hours of editing and retyping, and also dealt with my obsessing over the details.

I am also grateful for the dozens of hours of conversation we were able to share talking about all the different facets of life: leadership, business, relationships and of course the 5 C's and how they impact each of those. Tess and her husband Dean are an amazing resource, and they are also excellent friends.

I want to thank my business mentors Kenny Briggs, Terry Mayfield, and Greg Baker. These men have offered so much dedication, guidance, and perspective to me. They have helped set me on the path to becoming the businessperson and leader that I am today. They have set the example of what true leadership looks like, and their legacy will live on through every other leader they create in addition to me.

To my lovely wife, Nichole, who is my primary source of common sense. I am so grateful to be married to such a fun, and loving woman. You are the best wife and mom, and I realize I am so fantastically lucky to have you in my life.

I am grateful to my parents. They raised me in a loving home, and provided a firm foundation that I could build the rest of my life on. Thanks Mom and Dad.

Finally, I am thankful to God. I have pursued God with vastly varying levels of intensity over the last 35 years, but as my life has progressed, I have zero doubt that He has guided and watched over my family and me. We are in a wonderful situation in life now that I recognize was not created by my own hand.

QUOTES AND RESOURCES

PART 1

P. XIX   Michael Shermer commencement address to University of Texas. YouTube video, Adm. William H. McRaven, *Wall Street Journal* (September 20-21, 2014).

P. XX   Albert Camus, Alexandra Stoddard, *You Are Your Choices – 50 Ways to Live the Good Life* (New York: HarperCollins, 2007), p. 11.

P. 1   Aristotle (January 2015, www.goodreads.com).

P. 1   Concept of choices, Alexandra Stoddard, *You Are Your Choices – 50 Ways to Live the Good Life* (New York: HarperCollins, 2007).

P. 1. 2   Blogger story by James Clear, Team Sky (**JamesClear.com/marginal-gains).**

P. 2, 3   Concept of Marginal Gains, Jeff Olson, *The Sight Edge – Turning Simple Disciplines into Massive Success and Happiness* (Austin, TX: Greenleaf Book Group, 2013) p. 11.

P. 3   Jim Rohn (January 2015, www.goodreads.com).

P. 5   Concept of Habits, Charles Duhigg, *The Power of Habit – Why We Do What We Do In Life And Business* (New York: Random House, 2012), pages 17-23.

P. 5   Charles Reade (January 2015, Wikipedia.org).

P. 5   Jim Rohn (January 2015, www.goodreads.com).

P. 6   Elbert Hubbard (www.kimbyrns.ca/accordingtokim/2015).

P. 7, 8   Stephen M. R. Covey, *The Speed of Trust, The One Thing That Changes Everything* (New York: Free Press, 2006), pages 19-26.

P. 7   Albert Einstein, Stephen M.R. Covey, *The Speed of Trust, The One Thing That Changes Everything* (New York: Free Press, 2006), p. 62.

P. 8   "*Catch Me If You Can*," 2003 Dreamworks movie. Adapted from book by Frank Abagnale Jr. and Stan Redding, *Catch Me If You Can: The Amazing True Story Of The Youngest And Most Daring Con Man In The History Of Fun And Profit* (New York: Random House, 1980).

P. 9   Stephen M.R. Covey, *The Speed of Trust, The One Thing That Changes Everything* (New York: Free Press, 2006), p. 62.

P. 13   John C. Maxwell, *The 21 Indispensable Qualities Of A Leader – Becoming the Person Others Will Want to Follow* (Nashville, TN: Thomas Nelson Publishers, 1999), p. 30.

P. 15   Martin Van Buren (January 2015, www.goodreads.com).

P. 15   Billy Joel (January 2015, www.izquotes.com).

P. 16   John Wooden (January 2015, www.brainyquote.com).

P. 17   Leadership and Management. Kouzes and Posner, *The Leadership Challenge* (San Francisco, CA: Jossey-Bass, 2002).

P. 17   Warren Bennis and Burt Nanus, *Leaders – Strategies For Taking Charge* (New York: HarperCollins, 2003), p. 20.

P. 18   Harry S. Truman (January 2015, www.truman.edu).

P. 23   Mike Krzyzewski, *Leading With The Heart, Coach K's Successful Strategies* (New York: Hachette Book Group, 2000), p. 49.

P. 23, 24   ibid., *Leading With The Heart, Coach K's Successful Strategies* (New York: Hachette Book Group, 2000).

P. 24   Charles Duhigg, *The Power of Habit – Why We Do What We Do In Life And Business* (New York: Random House, 2012), pages, xiv-xvi.

P. 25   Google's take on leadership (http://blog.idonethis.com/google-most-important-leadership-trait).

P. 27   Søren Kierkegaard (January 2015, www.mypdf.tisotry.com).

P. 28   Couch to 5K – C25K running program (January 2015, www.c25k.com).

P. 33   Julia Cameron, *The Artist's Way, A Spiritual Path to Higher Creativity* (New York: Penguin Putnam, 2002), p. 193.

P. 34   Johann Wolfgang Von Goethe (January 2015, www.brainyquote.com).

P. 34   *Tale of Two Sisters and an Orange* (March 2015, www.cramaswamy.wordpress.com).

P. 34, 35   Sir Richard Charles Nicholas Branson (May 2015, Wikipedia).

P. 35   Henry David Thoreau, David Keirsey, *Please Understand Me II* (Del Mar, CA: Prometheus Nemesis Book Company, 1998), p. xiii.

P. 36   James Kouzes and Barry Posner, *The Leadership Challenge* (New York: Jossey-Bass, 2002), p. 223.

P. 38   Eleanor Roosevelt (April 2015, www.quotes.net).

P. 43   Tess Cox (April 2015).

P. 47   Golda Meir (April 2015, www.wisdomquotes.com).

P. 49   Patrick Lencioni, *The Five Dysfunctions of A Team* (San Francisco, CA: Jossey-Bass, 2002), p. 40.

P. 50   Sigmoid Curve – Nature's timeline principle (Managetrainlearn.com).

P. 50, 51   Marcus Buckingham, *Stand Out* (Nashville, TN: Thomas Nelson, 2011), pages 5-6.

P. 52   Aristotle (April 2015, www.goodreads.com).

P. 54   Jim Rohn (January 2015, www.goodreads.com).

P. 56   Albert Einstein (April 2015, www.brainyquote.com).

P. 58   Jack Canfield, "*The Success Principles – How to Get from Where You Are to Where You Want to Be* (New York: HarperCollins, 2005), p. 342.

P. 58, 59   ibid., *The Success Principles – How to Get from Where You Are to Where You Want to Be* (New York: HarperCollins, 2005), p. 342.

P. 61   Peter M. Senge, *The Fifth Discipline – The Art & Practice of the Learning Organization* (New York: Double Day, 2006), p. 284.

P. 65   Max DePree, *Leadership is an Art* (New York: Dell Publishing Group, 1989), p. 64.

P. 68   Brene Brown, *Rising Strong – The Reckoning. The Rumble. The Revolution.* (New York: Spiegel & Grau, 2015), p. 8.

P. 71   Mark Victor Hansen, *"Put your future in good hands – your own."* (April 2015, www.brainyquote.com).

P. 73   James M. Kouzes and Barry Z. Posner, *Credibility – How Leaders Gain and Lose It – Why People Demand It* (San Francisco, CA: Jossey-Bass, 2011), p. 61.

P. 74, 75   Stephen R. Covey, *The 7 Habits of Highly Effective People* (New York: Free Press, 2004).

P. 74   ibid., *The 7 Habits of Highly Effective People* (New York: Free Press, 2004), p. 71.

P. 78   ibid., Johann Wolfgang von Geothe, Stephen R. Covey, *The 7 Habits of Highly Effective People* (New York: Free Press, 2004), p. 146.

P. 84   James M. Kouzes and Barry Z. Posner, *"Leadership Begins With an Inner Journey,"* essay in the journal Leader to Leader (Spring 2011, Leadertoleaderjournal.com).

P. 84, 85   Kerry Patterson, Joseph Grenny, David Maxfield, Ron McMillan, Al Switzler, *Influencer* (New York: McGraw-Hill, 2008), pages 13-14.

P. 86   James Kouzes and Barry Posner, *The Leadership Challenge* (New York: Jossey-Bass, 2002) p. 93.

P. 89   Kerry Patterson, Joseph Grenny, Ron McMillan, Al Switzler, *Crucial Conversations* (New York: McGraw-Hill, 2002), p. 193.

P. 89   Patricia Fripp (May 2015, www.fripp.com).

P. 90   Jim Rohn (January 2016, goodreads.com).

P. 93, 94   Kerry Patterson, Joseph Grenny, Ron McMillan, Al Switzler, *Crucial Conversations* (New York: McGraw-Hill, 2002).

P. 94   ibid., *Crucial Conversations* (New York: McGraw-Hill, 2002), p. 21.

P. 94   ibid., *Crucial Conversations* (New York: McGraw-Hill, 2002), pages. 1-2.

P. 94   Mark Goulston, *Discover The Secret To Getting Through To Absolutely Anyone, Just Listen* (New York: AMACOM, 2010), p. 29.

P. 93, 95   ibid., *Discover The Secret To Getting Through To Absolutely Anyone, Just Listen* (New York: AMACOM, 2010).

P. 98   Dale Carnegie (May 2015, www.brainyquote.com).

P. 100   The Arbinger Institute, *Leadership and Self-Deception* (San Francisco, CA: Berrett-Koeler, 2010), p. 15.

P. 102, 103 The Arbinger Institute (San Francisco, CA: Berrett-Koeler, 2010).

P. 105   Marshall Goldsmith, *What Got You Here Won't Get You There* (New York: HYPERION, 2007).

P. 105   Jim Rohn (January 2016, goodreads.com).

P. 106   Paul Hudson (June 2015, www.elitedaily.com).

P. 110   Robert Collier (June 2015, www.brainyquote.com).

P. 110   Capt. Chesley B. Sullenberger, *"Miracle on the Hudson."* (February 6, 2009 - www.youtube.com/watch?v=imDFSnklB0k).

P. 110   Malcolm Gladwell, *Outliers* (New York, NY: BACK BAY BOOKS, Little, Brown and Company, 2008).

P. 113   Bertie Charles (June 2015, www.izquotes.com).

P. 115   Gary Keller, *The ONE Thing* (Austin, TX: Bard Press, 2012), p. 92.

P. 115, 116 ibid., *The ONE Thing* (Austin, TX: Bard Press, 2012), p. 89.

P. 117   Ralph Waldo Emerson (June 2015, www.emersoncentral.com).

P. 118   C.S. Lewis (June 2015, www.goodreads.com).

P. 118   Mark Twain (June 2015, www.values.com).

P. 121   Stephen R. Covey (June 2015, www.goodreads.com).

PART 2

P. 123   Jack Welch (June 2015, www.psychologytoday.com).

P. 126   Roger Connors and Tom Smith, *fixit – Getting Accountability Right* (New York: Penguin, 2016), p. 68.

Pg. 145   James Kouzes and Barry Posner, *The Leadership Challenge* (New York: Jossey-Bass, 2002), p. 83.

P. 154, 155 Jim Collins, *Great by Choice* (New York: Harper-Collins, 2011), pages 136-137.

P. 156   John Wooden (June 2015, www.goodreads.com).

P. 170   Elizabeth Gilbert, *Big Magic, Creative Living Beyond Fear* (New York: Riverhead Books, 2015), p. 247.

PART 3

P. 172   Jack Nicklaus (July 2015, www.azquotes.com).

P. 173   Tess Cox and Dan Klawer (July 2015).

P. 174   *"Steve Ballmer Became a Rookie Basketball Mogul".* The New York Times by Monica Langley (August 25, 2014).

P. 178   Martin Luther King Jr. (July 2015, www.goodquotes.com).

PART 4

P. 197   Maya Angelou (July 2015, www.goodquotes.com).

Made in the USA
Middletown, DE
26 March 2017